WHERE WATER IS GOLD

LIFE AND LIVELIHOOD IN ALASKA'S BRISTOL BAY

CARL JOHNSON

BRAIDED RIVER

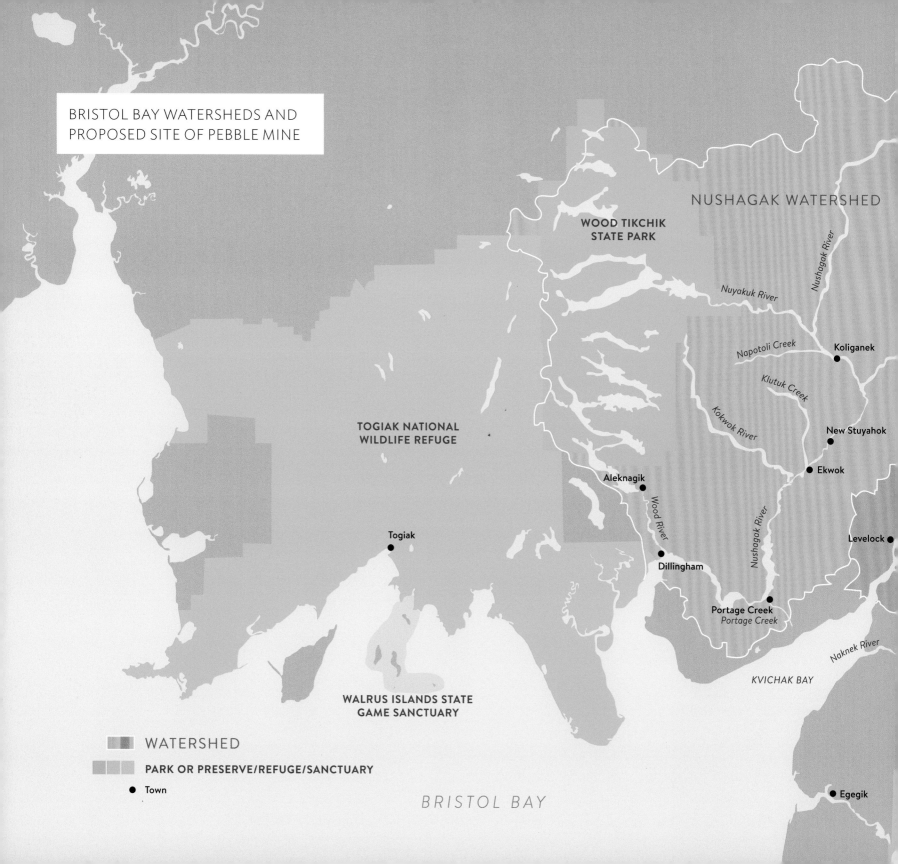

BRISTOL BAY WATERSHEDS AND
PROPOSED SITE OF PEBBLE MINE

NUSHAGAK WATERSHED

WOOD TIKCHIK
STATE PARK

Nushagak River

Nuyakuk River

Napotoli Creek   Koliganek

Klutuk Creek

Kokwok River

New Stuyahok

TOGIAK NATIONAL
WILDLIFE REFUGE

Aleknagik   Ekwok

Wood River

Togiak   Levelock

Nushagak River

Dillingham

Portage Creek
Portage Creek

WALRUS ISLANDS STATE
GAME SANCTUARY   Naknek River

KVICHAK BAY

WATERSHED

PARK OR PRESERVE/REFUGE/SANCTUARY

● Town

BRISTOL BAY   ● Egegik

MULCHATNA RIVER

CHULITNA RIVER

LAKE CLARK

LAKE CLARK NATIONAL
PARK AND PRESERVE

Port Alsworth

KOKTULI RIVER

PEBBLE MINE—
PROPOSED SITE

Nondalton

PILE RIVER

STUYAHOK RIVER

Iliamna

Newhalen

Pedro Bay

INISKIN BAY

Lower Talarik Creek

Upper Talarik

Newhalen

ILIAMNA LAKE

Kokhanok

KVICHAK RIVER

Iglugig

GIBRALTER LAKE

Dream Creek

COOK INLET

KVICHAK WATERSHED

ALAGNAK RIVER

KATMAI NATIONAL
PARK AND PRESERVE

BECHAROF
NATIONAL
WILDLIFE
REFUGE

Alaska

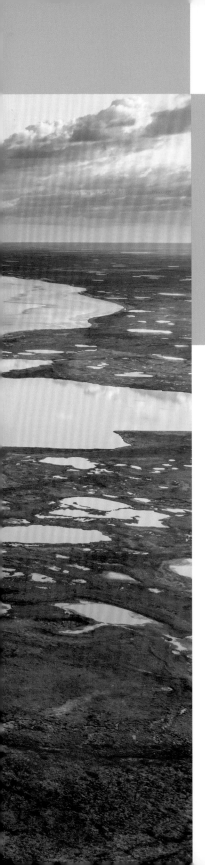

Sandra Day O'Connor

FOREWORD

For four decades, I have been an avid flyfisher. I have fished in solitude on small streams in Montana, and with my staff along the Potomac River, and in the wild, pristine country surrounding Bristol Bay in southwest Alaska.

Rivers with origins in the snow-covered peaks of the Aleutian and Alaska Range thread through tundra and wetlands to flow in massive braids into the largest wild Sockeye salmon fishery left on Earth.

The millions of salmon in Bristol Bay feed grizzlies, eagles, whales. They feed the Native communities who have called the region home for thousands of years and they feed people all around the world. Bristol Bay's fisheries account for 40 percent of the world's salmon.

Clouds and evening light reflect on a calm Iliamna Lake.

There have been—and will continue to be—unsustainable development plans for Bristol Bay. Threats to this region include large-scale mining proposals with attendant toxic chemicals, landscape-altering roads, and construction—all near, or actually in, highly sensitive rivers and streams, all in an earthquake-prone zone. Wherever there is gold, copper, and other valuable metals and minerals, there will be people tempted to cash in for short-term gains.

Although our lifestyles often require the development of resources, I believe that there are places that are too environmentally sensitive for mining or other unsustainable development to occur. One of these special places is Bristol Bay.

In Bristol Bay, we must take the long view. We must expand our concept of wealth, counting the riches of food for the community to be just as important, if not more important, than profits to shareholders. We must recognize that pristine water habitats—those that enable the richness of the Bristol Bay salmon runs and the productivity of the region's rainbow trout streams—possess a value that is immeasurable.

The hard work of a committed coalition of everyday Americans—conservationists, Alaska Native tribes and individuals, lodges, backcountry guides, anglers, commercial fishermen, restaurant owners, jewelers, recreationists, and others—has protected Bristol Bay. I have watched representatives from diverse industries work together to protect and celebrate this amazing place.

I invite you to turn the pages of this book and fall in love. Turn these pages and you, too, will understand why in Bristol Bay, it is water that is the true gold. ~

OPPOSITE *Backcountry travelers line kayaks up a stream in the Twin Lakes area of Lake Clark National Park and Preserve.*

RIGHT *Aerial view of an old cannery near the mouth of the Naknek River.*

BOTTOM LEFT *Light and shadow play on the surface of a small bay near the village of Togiak.*

BOTTOM RIGHT *Evening light splashes across a small stream.*

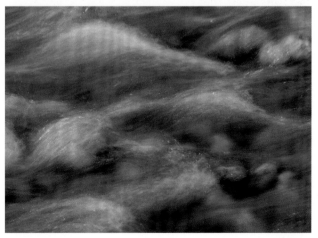

LEFT *A subsistence gill net extends out from Kanakanak Beach, catching Chinook and Sockeye salmon.*

RIGHT *A large raft of sea otters floats deep in Kukak Bay in Katmai National Park and Preserve.*

Bill Sherwonit

WHERE WATER IS GOLD

As measured on a map, Bristol Bay is not very far from Alaska's most highly developed and urbanized areas; parts of the region are within two hundred miles of Anchorage, a short hop by commuter plane. It is even closer to the Kenai Peninsula's cities, highways, and industries. In other ways, this large and bountifully wet section of Southwest Alaska is worlds apart. No highways exist, and hardly any roads (mainly dirt and gravel) extend beyond the edges of its thirty or so communities, most of which are small Native settlements. Few of the region's towns and villages have populations that exceed five hundred people; several have fewer than one hundred. The majority of residents have incomes that make them among the country's poorest. Yet as a whole, these "people of the salmon" consider their lives, like the place itself, to be remarkably rich.

Remnants of Libby's Koggiung Cannery near the mouth of the Kvichak River

Bristol Bay is home to about 7400 humans, spread across an area that encompasses around 46,000 square miles. That is larger than thirteen states in the Lower 48, with a density of about one person for every 5.5 square miles. When Bristol Bay's marine waters are added, the region more closely approximates the size of North Dakota or Washington, some seventy thousand square miles. The area has little infrastructure: few ports and no dams, no large power plants, no major utility corridors, no mines. It does have a relative abundance of airfields; air and water travel are the primary ways that people get around for much of the year. But most of these are small landing strips, with limited facilities. Only a few are able to accommodate large jets.

This paucity of people and infrastructure contributes greatly to Bristol Bay's true wealth: its natural abundance. Even in Alaska, few places are as pristine and richly wild. One measure of that wealth is the region's multitude of protected areas: two national parks, one national monument, and four national wildlife refuges (and these are just the federal units). Bristol Bay is also home to the nation's largest and wildest state park, a world-famous wildlife sanctuary, two game refuges, and five critical habitat areas. These parks and refuges are public lands, owned by and for the benefit of all of us. But this profusion of natural plenty is gravely threatened by corporate mining interests and other development—development that Bristol Bay fishermen and subsistence-dependent residents, most of them Alaska Natives (along with a diverse group of politicians, activists, sportsmen, and others) have made clear they do not want.

The variety of terrain and habitats is enormous. The Alaska Peninsula, which forms the bay's southern border, is part of the Pacific Rim's Ring of Fire. Nearly fifty volcanoes have been identified here, twenty of

them historically active. A half-dozen mountain ranges arc through the region; though not especially high, many peaks are ruggedly jagged and some are still being carved by alpine glaciers. Moving downhill from the highest elevations, glacial ice and bare rock become alpine tundra, which gives way to subalpine thickets, forested hills and flatlands, and moist tundra expanses that are part of a vast wetland system speckled by myriad ponds and lakes, including the nation's largest undeveloped lake, Iliamna. There are at least six major river drainages, with innumerable tributaries that rush and meander across the landscape and provide critical fish habitat. Offshore are several islands, some with high cliffs, used as rookeries by birds and haulouts by marine mammals.

More than 190 species of birds seasonally inhabit Bristol Bay, including millions of seabirds that congregate in one of the world's greatest concentrations of seabird colonies. According to Audubon Alaska, this "avian crossroads" is one of the single most important regions to bird populations on the planet— twenty-seven locales throughout Bristol Bay have been designated globally Important Bird Areas (IBAs). Coastal areas along the Alaska Peninsula provide critical habitat for the endangered Steller's eider, and six other species on Audubon's "Alaska WatchList" depend on Bristol Bay in some way.

In addition to birds, the federal government has identified seventeen marine mammals that may occur here "regularly or sporadically," including some endangered or threatened species. The bay is known for its walruses; each summer thousands of bulls famously gather at Round Island. Among the forty-one species of land mammals, however, no animal symbolizes Bristol Bay's natural richness more than its brown bears, which congregate in large numbers and impressive close quarters while feeding on an abundant, concentrated, and energy-rich food source: salmon. The largest male brown bears weigh a half ton or more.

But Bristol Bay's greatest treasures are its fish and the inland and marine waters that allow dozens of species to thrive, including many harvested in commercial, sport, and/or subsistence fisheries, such as halibut, herring, rainbow trout, northern pike, whitefish, Arctic char, Arctic grayling, lake trout, and Dolly Varden. What really defines this region and underscores its value are the five species of Pacific salmon—Chinook, Chum, Coho, Pink, and Sockeye—that return to Bristol Bay's river systems each year, an amazing spectacle in an age when many wild salmon runs around the world have been depleted, if not destroyed. Among the bay's most remarkable runs is the annual return of Chinook, or king, salmon to the Nushagak River and its tributaries. Largest of the Pacific salmon, the Nushagak's kings can weigh more than fifty pounds, to the delight of sport fishers. In recent years, while most of Alaska's king salmon streams have suffered dismal returns, the Nushagak has continued to meet and, in some instances, greatly exceed king salmon escapement goals; it has been described as the state's "top [Chinook] performer" and is among the world's greatest wild Chinook salmon rivers.

The fish for which Bristol Bay is most famous, however, is the Sockeye or red salmon. Not especially big, these Sockeyes average six to seven pounds, and they are enormously abundant. The region is home to the world's greatest wild run of Sockeyes. From 1963 to 2014 an average of 32.4 million reds returned to Bristol Bay's river systems. Long-term records show cyclical ups and downs, but the past decade has seen a Sockeye boom, with a ten-year average of 38.6 million fish and a projected return in 2015 of about 54 million—the most since 1995, when 60.8 million

adult Sockeyes swam home. While in the ocean, adult Sockeyes have silvery sides, white bellies, and blue-green backs. After reentering natal streams and lakes to spawn, they change dramatically: males grow large humped backs and the heads of both genders turn green while their bodies become a brilliant crimson (thus the nickname "reds"). In their prime, Sockeyes have an exceptionally tasty and nutritious reddish-orange flesh, a big part of their allure.

Nowadays, with most salmon runs elsewhere considerably diminished from historical highs because of pollution, overfishing, dam construction, loss of habitat, and other factors, Bristol Bay accounts for nearly *half* of the world's wild Sockeyes—an astonishing fact. The Institute of Social and Economic Research (ISER) of the University of Alaska at Anchorage reported in 2013 that the 2010 harvest, processing, and retail sales of Bristol Bay salmon—well over 90 percent of them Sockeyes—created $1.5 *billion* in sales value across the United States. But the worth of Bristol Bay's Sockeyes goes far beyond their commercial importance, however. Sockeyes are a keystone species in this region—crucial to the entire web of life. Annual spawning salmon bring millions of tons of marine nutrients to the area's nutrient-poor inland waters. Whether fresh or decayed, Sockeyes nourish a tremendous variety of organisms—from people and bears to insects and algae. They are an equally important food to certain fish, most notably the highly prized rainbow trout. Bristol Bay is home to the world's greatest population of large wild rainbow trout, and Sockeyes are the reason those rainbows are so plentiful. Rainbows may reach forty inches or longer; such "jumbos" have been the heart of a sport-fishing industry that in recent years has contributed $60 million or more annually to Alaska's economy.

LEFT *A greater yellowlegs wades through a pond in the Chigmit Mountains.* OPPOSITE *A group of black-legged kittiwakes nest in a rookery on the coast of Katmai National Park and Preserve.*

WHERE WATER IS GOLD

OPPOSITE *A brown bear
sow and her two yearling
cubs comb the shoreline in
Kukak Bay.*

Why is Bristol Bay so rich in Sockeyes? It begins with their preference to spawn along lakeshores and in tributaries that feed lakes. Given the bay's immense wealth of stream-linked ponds and lakes, big and small, the region is "Sockeye heaven." A rarity in other places, there is "lots and lots of natural, intact Sockeye habitat," says fisheries scientist Carol Ann Woody. These river-and-lake systems are clean and unaltered; no dams, no roads, no culverts or other human developments have damaged a system that has worked beautifully for millennia. Within this immense habitat, Sockeyes have evolved hundreds of distinct populations. Some, for example, spawn only in large lakes; others in tiny, shallow creeks. Each population has adapted to the specific conditions of its spawning area, each has its own life history. Such biodiversity occurs both within and among the bay's major drainages. Taken as a whole, it makes the entire system more stable and reliable. Scientists sometimes call this natural variation the "portfolio effect," nature's hedge against catastrophe. Such a buffering effect is enormously important in a system that has come to be exploited on an industrial scale. "It's remarkable that a place like this still exists," Woody says. Because of Bristol Bay's location in a remote, roadless part of Alaska, "Sockeye-wise, there's absolutely nothing like it."

A large majority of Bristol Bay's modern residents are Alaska Natives, whose ancestors settled in the region ten thousand or more years ago. Archeological records show that salmon have been an important part of their culture for at least four thousand years. Sockeyes are essential to subsistence culture, in ways not usually measured—or easily understood—by mainstream Americans. It is no exaggeration to say that the lives and lifestyles of most Alaska Natives in this region depend on salmon. Most of them are

Yup'ik Eskimos; others are Dena'ina Athabascans and Alutiiqs (in the past, commonly called Aleuts). Though each group has its own traditional social structure, cultural expressions, and homelands, there has been considerable mixing among Alaska Natives, as well as with non-Natives, in recent times. A subsistence lifestyle connects them all.

Many Bristol Bay residents (both Native and non-Native) participate in a mixed-cash economy: they depend to some degree on money, necessary to pay for such essentials of contemporary life as fuel, electricity, motorized transportation, plus some foods and other home supplies. But few can afford to pay for all their material needs, due primarily to high shipping costs, so they "live off the land" and its connected waters. Here, though, subsistence is much more than simply a method of harvesting wild foods; to Alaska Natives it is a way of life, with cultural, social, and spiritual elements that define how communities, families, and individuals behave among themselves and within the larger natural world.

Subsistence practices inform the knowledge, attitudes, beliefs, and even the identity of the region's Yup'ik, Dena'ina, and Alutiiq peoples. They reinforce key cultural values of respect and communal sharing, and inform Native peoples' sense of wealth. Tom Tilden, first chief of the Curyung Tribal Council, explains: "My grandmother used to say, 'We're so rich.' I would ask her why did she think we were rich and she would say because of the fish, birds, seals, berries—abundant foods that we harvest right here in Bristol Bay. She thought this was the richest place in the world." Residents harvest, consume, and celebrate a great variety of wild foods year-round—from moose to waterfowl, beluga whales to wild greens—but more than half of their diet is salmon, especially Sockeyes. These are among the world's last indigenous "salmon

people." Given the importance of salmon and other fish to the local subsistence-based cultures of Bristol Bay, it makes sense that water is also treated with a special reverence. As Yup'ik resident and activist Bobby Andrew once said: "Everything around us has life and must always be respected. Earth has life and its life blood is water, which flows underground just like a human being has blood vessels. Water provides life and without it we and all animals and fish cannot survive."

Bristol Bay has remained largely wild and undeveloped because, until recently, the region has never been targeted as a place rich in extractable resources such as oil or gold. That began to change in the late 1900s, however, with the promise of offshore oil and gas deposits. Economic interest on an industrial scale accelerated dramatically in the early 2000s, following the discovery of a huge copper-gold deposit. Serious interest in the region's oil and gas potential first emerged in the mid-1970s. Then governor Jay Hammond is credited with persuading the federal government to abandon any oil and gas leasing program because of the threat it could pose to valuable commercial fisheries and the region as a whole, but it was revived in the 1980s. In 1988 the Department of the Interior offered Lease Sale 92, encompassing 5.6 million acres in the North Aleutian Basin, along Bristol Bay's outer fringes. Eight oil companies bid $95 million for the rights to explore and develop the area.

Just months later, the Exxon *Valdez* ran aground in Prince William Sound. Both an ecological and social disaster, that oil spill prompted Congress to place a moratorium on any North Aleutian Basin resource development. The government bought back the leasing rights in 1995, and President Bill Clinton followed with an executive order protecting the area through 2012. All looked hopeful until Congress ended its

LEFT *Justin Pleier, crewman on the F/V Megan Dee, celebrates a large haul of herring.*

RIGHT *A drift commercial fishing boat lists to one side as it hauls in its catch.*

moratorium in 2003, and President George W. Bush cleared the way in 2007 for the area to be reopened to leasing. Lease Sale 214 was scheduled for 2011. Bolstered by President Barack Obama's election in 2008, fisheries and environmental advocates made a new push to protect Bristol Bay's waters. Presented with overwhelming opposition to the lease sale by the people of the region, President Obama canceled it in 2010 and extended protections through 2017.

Though encouraged, advocates for Bristol Bay's fisheries, waters, and Native communities felt greater safeguards were needed. More than fifty Alaska tribes and regional Native organizations and twenty seafood companies and commercial fishing associations requested permanent protection for Bristol Bay. So did the Fish Basket Coalition, an alliance representing Alaska Natives, commercial fishermen, conservationists, and local communities. Among their arguments: the region's fisheries produce 40 percent of the nation's annual wild seafood catch, valued at $2.5 billion; fish generally (and salmon especially) are the heart of the region's subsistence culture; and these waters and adjacent lands protect globally significant populations of seabirds, waterfowl, and marine mammals. The decades-long effort to protect the region was rewarded in late 2014. Citing the importance of Bristol Bay and the North Aleutian Basin Planning Area to subsistence use by Alaska Natives, wildlife, wildlife habitat, and sustainable commercial and recreational fisheries, and with a goal of ensuring that the unique resources of Bristol Bay remain available for future generations, President Obama announced his decision to permanently remove the North Aleutian Basin from future lease sales.

An even greater threat has loomed in recent years: economically valuable low-grade metal deposits, spread across the region beneath tundra wetlands and

WHERE WATER IS GOLD

OPPOSITE *Strips of drying
Sockeye salmon hang in a
smokehouse in Naknek.*
RIGHT *Tatiana Askoak
prepares Sockeye salmon
at her family's home in
Newhalen.*

hills near its two largest lakes, Iliamna and Clark. The
biggest and richest of these has been named the Pebble
deposit. The company that owns the rights to this rich
ore body—among the largest gold and copper deposits
in the world—has reported that its claims contain as
much as 55 billion pounds of recoverable copper, 3.3
billion pounds of molybdenum (a metallic element that
is used in strengthening steel), and 67 million ounces
of gold. At 2014 metal prices their combined estimated
value was more than $300 billion. If developed, the
Pebble Mine would be North America's largest gold
and copper mine, the chief gold producer in the world.
But billions of tons of rock would have to be removed
from the ground, with the "waste" stored in tailings
ponds behind large earthen dams. Construction of an
open pit mine, waste ponds, a hundred-mile road and
other mine-related infrastructure would destroy a large
swath of landscape and associated waters.

Scientists and residents have many concerns about
the proposed mine. But more than anything, the
inevitable seepage of acidic water and dissolved copper
into the tributaries of major salmon streams is cause
for alarm. As biologist Carol Ann Woody explains,
"Copper is one of the most toxic chemicals to aquatic
life." The threats to salmon, commercial fisheries, and
subsistence are why more than 70 percent of Bristol
Bay's residents and two-thirds of Alaskans oppose
development of the mine. Bob Waldrop, who's been
involved in Bristol Bay's commercial fisheries one way
or another since the 1970s, emphasizes that a long-
term perspective is necessary. If mining were allowed,
toxic wastes would remain long after the mine has
closed, essentially "in perpetuity—forever, till the sun
goes out." Given enough time, he believes, "something awful is going to happen." There is a choice to
be made, Waldrop continues: go with the short-term
economic boom, or protect a renewable, sustainable

treasure that has enriched Bristol Bay's people for
thousands of years and sustained a thriving commercial fishery for well over a century. "We truly have our
last chance to do it right *the first time*, at least involving salmon," he says. "It's a classic conflict, a fork in
the road. One path follows a renewable philosophy;
the other is an extraction philosophy, which is a one-
way street. If you take that fork, you can't go back. . . .
In the long run, the salmon will out-value the mine by
a huge amount. The locals, the Native peoples, they
understand this."

Vic Fischer, now in his nineties, understands this as
well as anyone. He was one of fifty-five delegates to
participate in the 1955 Alaska Constitutional Convention and hear the inspiring words of E. L. "Bob"
Bartlett. The territory's lone representative in Congress, Bartlett beseeched participants to pay special
attention to "the vital issues of resource policy."
Bartlett pointed to the history of both Alaska's mining
and commercial fishing industries as prime examples
of the "robber baron philosophy" and the "ruthless

plundering" of the territory's natural resources. He urged delegates to demonstrate "political maturity by giving notice that Alaska's resources will be administered, within the bounds of human limitations and shortcomings, for the benefit of all the people." The delegates took Bartlett's words to heart with Article 8 of the Alaska Constitution, which makes it clear that development of the state's resources would be for their "maximum use consistent with the public interest."

Applying these principles to Bristol Bay, Fischer asks, "What's in the public's best interest? Can the two [salmon versus mining development] co-exist? If not, which is more important? To my mind, you either have to find a way of living with both of them, or make sure that whatever is more important in the long run to the maximum benefit of the people now and in the future, that becomes the dominant concern and is sustained by public policy." From a constitutional perspective, Fischer maintains, state officials have so far failed their constitutional obligation to determine "what is the public interest here." That failure has rankled many Bristol Bay residents and is a primary reason that Native groups petitioned the federal Environmental Protection Agency to intervene in the Pebble dispute.

Robert Heyano, president of the United Tribes of Bristol Bay, wrote in 2015: "The Pebble Partnership cannot guarantee the safety for our fishery, and thus cannot ensure the continuation of our life. . . . We cannot afford this mistake—not when our very survival, our culture, and our livelihoods are on the line." Those who know Bristol Bay best understand that its greatest and sustainable, long-term wealth depends on the interplay of its two prime natural treasures: the salmon, of course, but also the region's clean and abundant waters. Water, as the late Bobby Andrew expressed it, is the lifeblood that sustains this place. More than anything else, that life-giving water must be protected if the salmon and the salmon people—and all other creatures living here—are going to thrive. ⌐

ABOVE *Protecting the marine waters of Bristol Bay helps protect salmon and our "fish basket."* (Graphic courtesy Fish Basket Coalition)

LEFT *Victor Fischer, one of two surviving delegates of the Alaska Constitutional Convention, was a plaintiff in a lawsuit challenging the Pebble exploration permits.*

The sky reflects on the calm surface of the Chulitna River within Lake Clark National Park and Preserve.

LEFT *Sockeye salmon in Iliamna
Lake* (Photo by Pat Clayton)
ABOVE *Sockeye salmon
in the Upper Nushagak River*
(Photo by Pat Clayton)

FROM NAKNEK TO PIKE PLACE

IN 2014 THE ENVIRONMENTAL PROTECTION AGENCY published its final watershed assessment conducted under the Clean Water Act. The report found that the proposed Pebble Mine development would adversely impact Sockeye salmon populations in Bristol Bay. US Senator Maria Cantwell of Washington issued a press release praising the findings. What was her interest in this issue that impacted waters 1600 miles to the northwest? Of course it's all about Pacific Northwest commercial fishing jobs.

At river mouths spread out over two hundred miles of coastline, commercial fishing boats swarm Bristol Bay each summer to catch nearly half of the world's Sockeye salmon supply. In 2014 that catch totaled over thirty million fish at an ex-vessel value of $200 million (NOAA defines this as "a measure of the dollar value of commercial landings, usually calculated as the price per pound at first purchase of the commercial landings multiplied by the total pounds landed"). According to the Alaska Commercial Fisheries Entry Commission, nearly 35 percent (some 645 out of 1,855) of commercial drift gill net permit holders are from the state of Washington. Total gross earnings and labor income earned by Washington residents in all Alaska fisheries is estimated annually at $1.04 billion and $471 million, respectively. Almost all major seafood processing companies involved in the Bristol Bay fishery are based in Seattle. Many of the drift commercial Sockeye salmon permit holders in Bristol Bay spend their winters in Seattle while their boats sit out the winter in Naknek, one of the bay's two main fishing hubs. When the time comes, they fly up to the small logistical hub of King Salmon and get their boats ready for another season. Sometime in mid- to late July, depending on how good the season was, they catch a flight back to Anchorage and continue on home to Seattle.

Seattle also provides a vibrant consumer market ready to purchase and enjoy all manner of Alaska's seafood. Downtown Seattle's famous Pike Place Market showcases plenty of fresh seafood from the state—halibut, Sockeye (red) and Chinook (king) salmon, and king crab. In early May large banners celebrate the coming Copper River Sockeye salmon opener, while other signs tout Alaska's clear, clean, and fresh waters and the associated quality of seafood that comes from it. Alaska's seafood is an economic engine in Washington State, directly employing over eighteen thousand people—from restaurants and grocers to suppliers and seafood industry workers—for a total labor income of over $1 billion in 2011. The seafood industry produced eight thousand *indirect* jobs in the same year. Seattle is a key player in the global market, as the second-most important export location for Alaska's seafood (behind Anchorage), according to NOAA Fisheries. ⌐

From Pike Place Market, Seattle:
OPPOSITE *Wild Alaskan Sockeye salmon for sale*
ABOVE *View from a produce stand*
RIGHT *Crab from the "clear waters of Alaska"*

RIGHT *Alaskan wild Chinook salmon at Pike Place Market*
BELOW *View of Seattle Center and downtown Seattle with Mount Rainier in the distance*

OPPOSITE *Mount Redoubt, an active stratovolcano in the Aleutian Range, catches the morning light.*
ABOVE *A harbor seal pup rests on a rock in Kukak Bay.*

OPPOSITE *Fall colors along the braided portion of the Kvichak River*
ABOVE *Pond and wetlands in between the Kvichak and Naknek rivers*

FOLLOWING PAGE, LEFT *A young brown bear boar wades through wetlands on the edge of the Brooks River.*
FOLLOWING PAGE, RIGHT *A small stream flows into Frying Pan Lake, the headwaters of the South Fork Koktuli River.*

LEFT *Caribou antler and fireweed in a patch of lowbush cranberries*
ABOVE *Old guns decorate the wall of a home in Igiugig.*

ABOVE *The residents of the village of Iliamna call this peninsula "The Rock."*
OPPOSITE *Tent at a campsite in the Twin Lakes area of Lake Clark National Park and Preserve*

FOLLOWING PAGE, LEFT *Steam rises from Mount Redoubt, an active stratovolcano, with Mount Iliamna in the background.*

FOLLOWING PAGE, TOP RIGHT *Fossilized leaves in sandstone along the coast of Katmai National Park and Preserve*
FOLLOWING PAGE, BOTTOM *A young red fox rests along the shore amidst a patch of barnacles and blue mussels.*

ABOVE *Semipalmated plover*
on alpine tundra in the
Chigmit Mountains
OPPOSITE *Alpine lupine decorates*
the coastline in Kukak Bay.

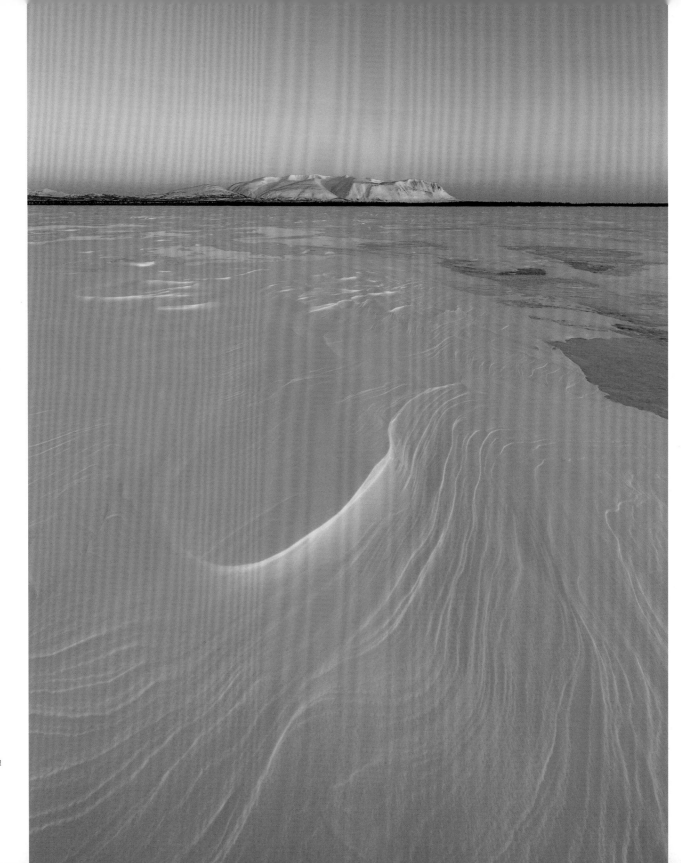

OPPOSITE *A brown bear boar sits at the base of Brooks Falls looking for Sockeye salmon.*
RIGHT *Snow drifts on a frozen Sixmile Lake with the Chigmit Mountains in the background.*

LEFT *Commercial fishing boats in Kulukak Bay at dusk*
RIGHT *Alutiiq artist Peter Lind holds one of his works, a traditional hunter's visor.*

FOLLOWING PAGES, LEFT *Russian Orthodox crosses adorn the cemetery at the village of Igiugig.*
RIGHT *Evening light catches the St. Nicholas Chapel in the village of Igiugig.*

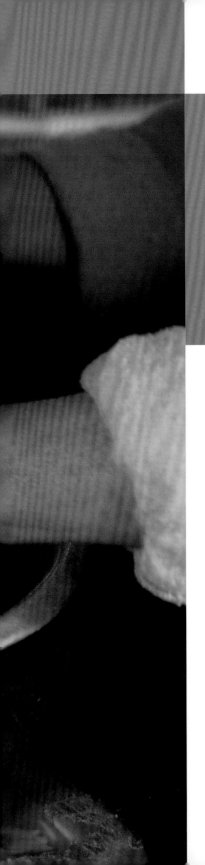

Anne Coray and Steve Kahn

MOVING WITH THE SEASONS

Before there were clocks and watches and modern calendars, the Dena'ina, Yup'ik, and Alutiiq peoples of Southwest Alaska relied on the seasons and natural cycles to tell time. There was the sun, moving from east to west every day; the rising and falling of tides; the moon, waxing and waning monthly; the snows and ice to signify winter; the spring melts; the long warm days of summer; the reds and yellows and frosts that meant autumn was in full swing. There were animals like bears that disappeared during hibernation; others like the weasel that changed color. There were bird and waterfowl migrations; there were salmon swimming up streams to spawn. This was how time was measured. These cycles were constant, ushering in familiar changes to the landscape, changes that could be counted on and that always came full circle.

A pair of Dena'ina women cut smoked salmon strips for canning.

Nashookpuk of Naknek, stitch together beautiful traditional parkas. Other coastal residents create intricate coil baskets from wild rye grasses or carve ivory figurines. But whatever the activity—beachcombing for ivory, cutting alder for smoking fish, trapping beaver and muskrat, gathering sourdock or wild celery, picking salmonberries or blueberries—subsistence requires an understanding of the patterns of nature, knowledge of when animals or plants are in their prime.

As a subsistence user myself, I rely on these precious gifts from the land and water. It is like having a grocery store in your backyard. As non-Natives, my husband, Steve, and I do not have the right to hunt marine mammals, but our diet does consist largely of fish and game, and we heat our cabin exclusively with wood. We live on Lake Clark, on property that came by way of my parents, John and Claudine Coray, who acquired the land in the 1950s. I marvel daily at my good fortune.

For over two decades, during three or four weeks in July and August, Steve and I have gillnetted for red salmon from our beach. What we can't eat fresh we process in glass jars, using an old-fashioned wood cookstove to bring the pressure cooker up to temperature and maintain that heat for the required processing time. Salmon and firewood are without doubt the two natural resources we rely on most heavily, but since living at Lake Clark year-round, Steve and I have also fished for grayling, lake trout, burbot, and pike. We have taken five moose, two black bear, one caribou, and countless spruce grouse. Much of the game meat that we did not share with neighbors ended up in jars. We do not have a freezer or even twenty-four-hour power. It is a lot of work, and I once found myself grumbling, "I feel like I'm married to moose"— but the payoff is supply for a year or more of lean, hormone-free meat that makes dinners a snap: we simply

Today there are few places left on the planet where natural rhythms dominate. But the Bristol Bay region—covering 46,000 square miles and including portions of both the Alaska and Aleutian Ranges as well as seven of Alaska's largest lakes—gives us a glimpse of what life was like for indigenous peoples thousands of years ago. The people here are very much in tune with animal migrations and behavior, and they are still largely dependent on the land. That is why the term "subsistence" has assumed a special meaning and importance in the forty-ninth state.

Simply defined, "subsistence" is "the gathering and harvesting of natural resources," but most Alaska Natives and rural residents see it as a way of life. That means making use of salmon, wild game, berries, marine and fur-bearing mammals, waterfowl, bird eggs, wild plants, and firewood where available. Often resources provide sustenance, but sometimes they are used for ceremonial or handicraft purposes. Many women practice the fine art of skin sewing, making dolls, dance fans, and mukluks. Some, like Rhonda

open a jar and stir it in with some boiled pasta and kale or chard from the garden, and we have an instant stir-fry.

Our garden is bountiful. I'm grateful to the salmon, whose spawned-out carcasses we collect in the fall and bury whole for fertilizer. There is nothing like nutrients from fish, coupled with stove ash and burnt bones from the game we harvest, to produce gargantuan-sized greens. In spring, nature provides her own greens: fireweed shoots, wild beach onions, and fiddlehead ferns. Then come the berries. The first to ripen are currants, red translucent globes that we plop into pails in early August. Tart and juicy, they make a fantastic jelly. By the end of the month the tundra is awash in blueberries, my favorite for jam. In late September we pick lowbush cranberries, which we mash and simmer into juice loaded with vitamin C. August and September, months that typically see more rain, are times to scour the woods for mushrooms; Steve and I have identified and eaten goat's beard, oysters, and horse mushrooms as well as several species of *Agaricus*. The excellent flavor and added protein of wild mushrooms are a welcome supplement to our diet.

I find it humorous when people who are not familiar with our subsistence lifestyle ask, "What do you *do* out there?" My best answer: we practice freedom from corporate control of our food. Tatiana Askoak, of the village of Newhalen, agrees. "We're able to have control of the quality," she says, while expertly filleting a Sockeye (red salmon) for the smokehouse. There is nothing like wild Alaska salmon; the fish in and around Bristol Bay are not farmed or artificially bred and hatched. While the nutritional value of wild versus farmed fish is hotly debated, wild salmon generally win out, with more minerals and a lower risk of contaminants. As for hatchery-bred salmon, they often put wild

LEFT *A garden of greens at the Coray homestead on Lake Clark*

stocks at risk, sometimes mating with them and diluting their local adaptations and resistance to parasites and disease. I consider myself unbelievably lucky to live in a time and place where this embodiment of the natural world—the salmon's life cycle—is still relatively pristine.

Living so close to the land has made me appreciate even more the knowledge of traditional cultures, how the patterns of subsistence practices are etched in their bones. The Native people here know that walrus are the fattest in the fall, that the roots of the Eskimo potato are sweetest after a frost, that in the heart of winter beaver pelts are thickest and provide the most warmth for clothing. As a consequence of being dependent on the natural world, Steve and I too find ourselves thinking seasonally, in terms of harvest. We are aware that the calendar in our heads is three-dimensional, and far more complex than the one hanging on the wall. Like me, Steve was born and raised in Alaska. He feels privileged to have grown up on wild game meat, learning from a young age how to properly skin and butcher an animal. When speaking of hunting and fishing, he is respectful of both the game and the practices used for harvest.

Anne is right. For me, treating the land and animals appropriately is an imperative, passed down from my personal teacher, my father. As a boy I watched him skin and butcher many moose before I stood over my first, taken when I was eleven years old. Although my blood-stained knife laid back the hide, the real work—quartering, butchering, packing—was handled by adults. A caribou and a black bear followed, always with my father providing direction. When the time came for me to face the job alone, I was well prepared. I understand when Rick Delkittie of Nondalton says, "In the Dena'ina way, you learn from your uncles . . . I was really fortunate, I had lots of uncles."

There is no cultural divide when it comes to recognizing that the wisdom of our forebears is something to cherish and pass on to future generations. Though my personal journey with subsistence lifeways has meandered through the worlds of commercial and sport hunting and fishing, the shift to subsistence alone was a satisfying and complete conversion. I was happy to take my backcountry skills with me and leave behind an increasing sense of competition. Above all, I value the spirit of subsistence, which is sharing. Indigenous cultures commonly distribute bounties of fish and game with neighbors and family who are unable to harvest for themselves because of disability, age, or other circumstances. But as Anne pointed out, subsistence is about more than sustenance for the body. Traditional foods and handicrafts are also used during potlatches, weddings, funerals, dances, and other ceremonial occasions.

Rural residents in the Bristol Bay region often live by combining wild resource harvests with wage employment (often referred to as a mixed-cash economy). Under current state and federal laws and regulations, exchanges of subsistence-caught fish and wildlife involving cash may constitute customary trade as long as exchanges are limited and noncommercial. It is commonly thought that money is not a part of traditional subsistence economies, but for years Bristol Bay residents have needed cash to purchase basic necessities like fuel oil, gasoline, clothing, electricity,

and tools. Many of these tools are used for harvest. To practice subsistence, people use small-scale, appropriate technology: fishing nets, guns, ammunition, snowmachines, and aluminum skiffs with outboard motors. But just having the proper tools is not enough. Subsistence users have to know how and when to

use them. They understand the necessity of paying attention and seizing opportunities for gathering and harvesting when they appear.

As winter approaches and the time comes for me to fill out a hunting report, I am certain that my laugh echoes in Igiugig, Naknek, and Pedro Bay. "How many

The moon rises over the Chigmit Mountains and Lake Clark.

Nine-year-old Aiden Wassillie of Igiugig looks out on the frozen Iliamna Lake while hunting for snowshoe hare and willow ptarmigan.

That when fall nights grow cool, grouse will begin flocking to the beach to peck gravel for their gizzards.

But what once was familiar and reliable runs the risk of becoming strange and less predictable because of the uncertainties of climate change. As these weather shifts usher in unusual winter warm spells or make October feel like the month of August, we no longer know if we can count on seasonal patterns. In one of her poems, Anne asks, perhaps more as a rallying cry than a question: *Who knows when the swag-bellied bear / will cease its hibernation / the ptarmigan and weasel / dull to a twelve-month brown?* When natural cycles face threats, when the pages from the calendar in your head are ripped out and turned upside down from climate change, or when offshore drilling and large-scale mining loom like a big bad bruise on the horizon, a community of necessity is born. Disparate notions of politics, religion, borders, and race meld and strengthen into a common purpose: to form a vibrant social and cultural backbone of protection for Bristol Bay.

Yup'ik elder Tim Wonhola from Dillingham and New Stuyahok says, "We hunt on it, walk on it, swim in it; the land becomes part of us and we become part of it." When the interlocking network of the seasons, the movements of animals, the flourishing and withering of plants is part of your heritage, your daily footsteps and breath, it is second nature to consider the land and waters around you as kin. Protecting resources becomes just like protecting family. ⌇

days did you hunt?" the questionnaire asks. If the larder is low on game meat and the season is open—all of them! Picking berries, cutting wood, or walking on the beach are reasons to be in the land, taking in changes in temperature and precipitation, studying tracks, and looking for animal movements. Subsistence users are always recording things, and these mental notes often end up in casual conversations. Over a steaming mug of coffee, a neighbor relays news from downriver or across the bay that the Sockeyes are in the Kvichak. Or that Billy saw caribou on the Mulchatna. Or that blueberries are big and juicy because of last winter's snow. When you live in harmony with seasonal shifts, you know that when snow patches shrink in the woods, you will soon find tight spirals of fiddleheads periscoping up through the mounds of last year's dead stalks.

Anne Coray

HOMING NORTH

From Aleknagik up
The lakes form a winding stair,
A rise and run joined by rivers:
Agulowak. Agulukpak, Wind.

So the salmon swim from Bristol Bay
Return in summer to spawn, some
As far as Lake Kulik. To live

Is to climb, rails of land on either side,
Bend of Jackknife, Frog Mountains.
A winding stair, lake to lake, forget
The names, they swim to spawn,

Returning is all, in summer, this fever,
This homing north to find their
Creek, their bay, their mouth, the one

They were born to, to which they
Turn, again, again, and climb
And swim, and do not mourn,
Reddening, softening. Until.

A stream flows into Lower Twin Lake in Lake Clark National Park and Preserve.

Jack Hobson

A vocal Pebble Mine opponent, Jack takes a moment to record notes at a family hunting cabin.

Jack Hobson is a commanding presence in the backcountry. While he had the opportunity to see the world while in service with the US Marines, he was drawn back home to Nondalton. "It's a tough lifestyle," Jack notes, talking about the subsistence way of life. Going out with him in the backcountry, you quickly see that he is a hard worker and that he takes great pride in a successful moose hunt, a good day fishing, or a long day cutting salmon strips. Learning from his uncles, as is traditional for the Dena'ina people, he joined elders on hunting or fishing trips with nothing more than a sleeping bag when he was as young as five years old. He learned early how to run the river, so that in his forties he runs the river with the engine on full step at night, with no flashlight or flood light. Deeply invested in the subsistence lifestyle, he expresses great concern about how the chemicals involved in hard rock mining will affect the water that is integral to the ecosystem near his home. Given the high risk associated with mining, he cannot fathom jeopardizing the resources that he and his people have relied on for generations in exchange for the short term gain in the form of jobs. He notes that with the high cost of living in the area, it is even more important to have the abundance of renewable resources: "My uncle said out here that you would never go hungry unless you didn't know how to hunt or something." ～

OPPOSITE *The sun rises over scattered ice on the Nushagak River in early winter.*

TRADITIONAL TECH

ONE OF THE MOST EFFICIENT MEANS of harvesting large volumes of fish is through the use of a gill net. A set net from the beach is stretched out at low tide with an anchor on one end and a buoy on the other. The tide comes in, and fish are caught in the net. One can also set net or drift a gill net from a boat. The key to the effectiveness of a gill net is that it remains extended in length, with the bottom of the net weighed down by a lead line or groundline and the top kept afloat by a floatline (upper line or headrope). The mesh size (the size of the gap in between the lines of the net) determines what species are being targeted by the net.

But how does one catch fish with such a vital tool in the winter time, when the fish are under three or more feet of ice? How does one keep the net stretched out so that it is functional yet accessible under the ice, so it can be retrieved frequently to harvest fish? The genius of the jiggerboard solves that problem. What folks in Canada call an "ice jigger" or "prairie jigger," the people of Bristol Bay call a jiggerboard. Constructed of a long piece of slotted wood, with levers and hooks contained within the open slot of the board, the jiggerboard is placed in a hole under the ice. Using rope to pull the levers, which causes the hooks to dig into the ice above the board, the jiggerboard can be guided under the ice to a desired destination.

In the village of Nondalton, which sits on Sixmile Lake on the edge of Lake Clark National Park and Preserve, the primary winter fish to harvest is whitefish, along with lake trout and burbot. Residents cut two holes in the ice, far enough apart from one another to accommodate the length of the gill net. The jiggerboard is placed through one hole, attached to a line, and guided under the ice to the other hole. Once there, it can be pulled up and out, with the attached line now stretching under the ice. A gill net is then tied to the line and pulled from the first hole to the second. With a gill net in place under the ice, residents check the net every couple of days to gather any fish caught in the net. It is an efficient means of harvesting, allowing time for other winter tasks such as trapping, hunting, and splitting wood for the wood-burning stove. ∾

ABOVE *Picking fish from a gill net in the winter time can be cold on the hands.*
LEFT *Charles Balluta stretches out a gill net to ready it for reinsertion under the ice.*

OPPOSITE *Anastasia Hinkle pulls whitefish from a gill net on the frozen Sixmile Lake.*
LEFT *Nondalton residents work together to set a gill net under the ice to catch whitefish.*
RIGHT *Bob Tracey holds a jiggerboard.*

LEFT *A collection of red fox pelts hang on the wall of a cabin.*
OPPOSITE *Pete Caruso of King Salmon holds a trap he commonly uses for trapping fur-bearing animals.*

LEFT *Nondalton resident Jack Hobson checks for moose above the Chulitna River during the autumn hunt.*

RIGHT *A set of moose antlers adorns the face of an old building at a placer mining camp.*

OPPOSITE *A traditional cache for storing supplies sits on a homestead on the shore of Lake Clark.* RIGHT *Morning colors light up the sky over a float plane at the Coray homestead.*

Colors of fire blaze across the sky as the sun sets over the Chigmit Mountains.

RIGHT, TOP *Cut filets of salmon hang in a smoke house in Dillingham.* BOTTOM *A mixture of Chinook and Sockeye salmon, caught in a set gill net on Kanakanak Beach near Dillingham, awaits harvest.*

OPPOSITE, LEFT *Anne Coray checks the wild onions growing on the Lake Clark shoreline near her homestead.*
OPPOSITE, RIGHT *Steve Kahn tends the tomato plants in his greenhouse on Lake Clark.*
RIGHT *A variety of lettuce offer fresh greens for the table at the Coray homestead.*

LEFT *Hoar frost, the sure sign of a cold winter day, covers the ground.*
ABOVE *Ice floats by the banks of the Kvichak River on a winter morning.*

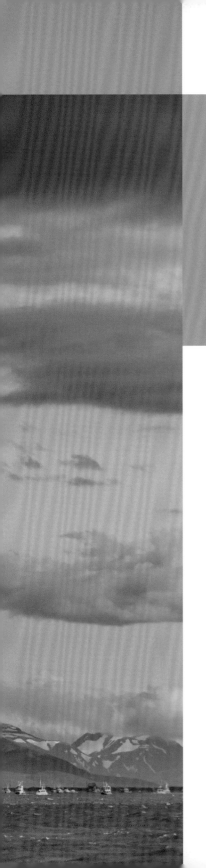

Dave Atcheson

A FIRESTORM OF ACTIVITY

L ife within the Bristol Bay basin takes a sudden and drastic turn about the same time each year, when coastal villages from Egegik to Dillingham emerge from winter's enduring hold to once again embrace the sudden spark of energy that ignites the entire region. More than just a wholesale case of spring fever, it is a pent-up sense of expectation, an almost instinctual force that spurs this annual firestorm of activity. As the last vestiges of snow and ice dissipate, empty harbors and abandoned processing plants, for months little more than ghost towns, fill with an urgency. There is a sudden fervor as dockside forklifts scurry and the extended arms of cranes shudder back to life, feeding a long line of vessels gearing up for the frenzy of the season ahead.

A fleet of commercial fishing drift boats converges at the mouth of the Ugashik River to deliver its catch.

of anticipation, waiting for the miracle of the Sockeye descending upon the bay in unimaginable numbers—often thirty million to fifty million strong. The essence of this place is transformed, engulfing visitors and residents alike in one of nature's great spectacles.

Yet it all starts far upstream and in relative quiet. After extended months of darkness, the billions upon billions of salmon eggs that have gestated under layers of gravel and ice begin to show new signs of life. It is a peaceful start in comparison to the fury of activity these hatchlings will soon trigger, a feeding frenzy among gulls and returning waterfowl as well as the other fish (rainbow trout, lake trout, and Dolly Varden) that depend on them. In the case of Sockeyes, the most numerous of the five species of salmon that call Bristol Bay home, the newly emerged fingerlings make their way upstream to one of the innumerable lakes that color this glorious, water-laden terrain. After up to two years there, they emerge and head down river as smolt, touching off another feeding frenzy on their way, before embarking on an even more perilous journey out to sea. Though only a small percentage of Sockeyes eventually return, they number in the tens of millions, many making their way back to the very streams of their birth, to spawn, lay eggs, and begin the process anew.

After spawning they die, giving the ultimate sacrifice: their demise feeds this ongoing ritual of regeneration and rebirth. Their decaying flesh provides food for their offspring, perpetuating their own species. It nourishes the vegetation along these rich and fecund streams, which indirectly feeds such animals as caribou and moose that feast on the rich plant life they fertilize. The Sockeyes provide sustenance to so many others: bears and wolves, other fish, and people—the people of Bristol Bay, the rest of Alaska, the Lower 48, and the larger world.

Populations burgeon as airplanes deposit fishermen from all corners of Alaska and from throughout the Pacific Northwest on these small, sometimes unpaved, landing strips. Accompanying them are an army of fresh-faced, wide-eyed world travelers—some coming for adventure, others simply to make wages in the processing plants or aboard boats, working beside villagers and the longtime hands who return, just like the fish, season after season. All arrive in a whirlwind

Perhaps what makes this process all the more
astounding—especially in the face of the collapse of
comparable fisheries throughout Europe, the East
Coast, and the Pacific Northwest—is the incredible
diversity this fishery maintains. Bristol Bay is one of
the last remaining strongholds for wild salmon because
the various populations of each species overlap and
return in intervals throughout the season, with each
run having adapted over thousands of years to its
particular home. Whether the largest river or tini-
est trickle, these streams run their serpentine course
through this vast landmass like capillaries in a massive
circulatory system. Many of them eventually filter their
way downstream into the great arteries of such rivers
as the Nushagak and Kvichak as well as into a series
of other smaller, though no less important, waterways
that eventually flow into Bristol Bay.

The complex web of genetic diversification is the
salmon's greatest asset in this perpetual drama that
plays out year after year, season after season. If one
piece of this intricate puzzle doesn't fair well in a given
summer, the others make up for it. Conversely, if even
a part of this system were to be corrupted, its arteries
severed—whether through habitat degradation, indus-
trialization, or the development of mining—the whole
would be significantly compromised, putting the entire
population at risk. This may be the last, and certainly
the best, representation of an intact and healthy fishery, having evolved over the millennia.

The Bristol Bay watershed envelops Alaska Native
subsistence users, rural residents, and commercial
fishermen—one of whom is Katherine Carscallen.
A striking young female skipper, Kat might not at
first glance fit the mold of a rough and tumble Bristol Bay boat captain, but she was born to fish. Kat's
mother skippered her own vessel, as did her father.

Her parents actually met on the fishing grounds and
eventually teamed up, and as a teenager Kat diligently
worked the deck of her father's boat. "It might just
have been a way to make money at first," she says,
"but later on I really began to appreciate the freedom
it allowed me, and as I built confidence in what I was
doing and had my own ideas on how things should be
run, it only seemed natural to get my own boat." Kat
looks forward to the mayhem of the season, the excite-
ment of getting her vessel ready, preparing her three- to

five-man crew, and the incredible burst of adrenaline when she is finally allowed to lay her nets out on the first day. Bristol Bay is one of the fastest paced and most competitive fisheries in Alaska.

"Being aware of what's happened (or almost happened) in the past," Kat says, "makes it something I don't take for granted." She is referring to the wide fluctuation that salmon numbers have taken since the first canneries appeared in the mid-1800s. From fish traps owned by large processing companies placed right in river mouths, to the wholesale slaughter caused by nonstop fishing, salmon populations have plummeted several times over the previous century. Those same conglomerates that owned the processing plants were the same ones that pushed a law in 1922 requiring all fishing to be done by sailboats. Masquerading as a conservation measure, it was really a means of keeping the fishermen tied to these corporate interests, fishing out of company-owned boats that often were towed to the fishing grounds. These practices continued for nearly thirty years, until 1951, when power boats were finally allowed.

With the introduction of power boats, there was a continual uptick in the number of independent fishermen but also a significant increase in harvest. This rise, combined with the introduction of nylon gill nets and a steep upturn of high-seas fishing by foreign nations, exacted an enormous toll on these fish stocks. Unfortunately, at that time escapement goals (the number of fish allowed to reach their natal streams to spawn) were not yet clearly formulated nor implemented, though progress was slowly being made. Salmon management took a giant step forward with Alaska statehood in 1959. Along with a constitution that included a mandate to conserve important natural resources, control of the fishery was transferred to state authority and henceforth handled locally.

Decorations in a workshop in Naknek express the owner's views on protecting Bristol Bay.

Improved methods of counting fish, escapement goals, and consistent management plans were gradually generated. By the 1970s limited entry was instituted, which controlled the number of fishermen allowed to participate in Bristol Bay, and a two-hundred-mile limit was imposed on foreign fishing vessels.

Currently the Bristol Bay management area (nearly the size of Ohio) is divided into five districts, corresponding to eight major river systems. The state Department of Fish and Game uses sophisticated

Workers process Sockeye salmon filets at Naknek Family Fisheries.

computer models and has been given expanded over-sight. Today Bristol Bay is touted by many as a model for other fisheries, but there is, nevertheless, a looming threat hanging heavy on the minds of many fishermen. The possibility of oil and gas exploration in the bay and mining inland, and the knowledge of what has occurred to fisheries elsewhere, has spurred activism. Kat, who began volunteering at a young age, says, "Initially it was just something to fill time during the off season and it seemed like the right thing to do, but after we began hearing about [the threat of the] Pebble Mine, it became imperative: we had to do something."

Kat works full time with such groups as Trout Unlimited and Commercial Fishermen for Bristol Bay in an effort to thwart the mining project. Yet, it is not just Pebble they are worried about: several other large companies hold mining claims in the area, so Kat and other fishermen-turned-activists know that Pebble is

The Bristol Bay salmon fishery is an enormous economic engine that has a ripple effect throughout the country. Astonishingly, the region accounts for nearly *half* of the world's wild Sockeyes. About half of the salmon catch, totaling over thirty million fish in 2014, is exported to Japan and throughout Asia. Much of the rest is sent to the West Coast and reprocessed, later sold as fillets or in cans across the United States and overseas. The value of the Sockeye returns is most dramatically revealed by their economic worth. For example, the 2010 harvest, processing, and retail sales of Bristol Bay salmon (more than 90 percent of them Sockeyes) created $1.5 billion in sales value across the United States. The commercial catch of over thirty million Sockeyes supported twelve thousand seasonal workers, and the direct value to fishermen of $165 million equaled nearly one-third of Alaska's total salmon harvest value and more than the total fish harvests (of *all* species) in forty-one other states.

The offshore fisheries of Bristol Bay—huge cash crops such as pollock, cod, and halibut that are shipped worldwide—depend on an inshore ecosystem that remains healthy. Also relying on clean water are the herring, whose golden caviar is harvested in a barrage each spring and exported almost exclusively to Japan. It is an important inshore fishery that many villagers as well as seasonal transplants rely upon for its injection of cash into the economy, and for fishers it is their first chance at getting on the water each year and earning an a living. Most important, as Kat and other Bristol Bay fisherman would remind us, the Bristol Bay watershed and its intricate and miraculous fishery is completely sustainable. It has fed us for generations. Despite the commercial fishery's ups and downs, this healthy and prolific resource will continue to sustain us for centuries to come only if we take care of it and continue to manage it properly. ∼

just the beginning. Development of resources would set a dangerous and perhaps irreversible precedent. "If they are allowed to begin the construction of a large open pit mine," she says, "the others, who are just waiting to see the outcome, would immediately follow, turning the richest fishery on the planet into a massive mining district." There are also more distant threats. Much of the land in the region, including some along major rivers, is within the jurisdiction of the Bureau of Land Management. While this land is currently not open for mining, under different federal leadership it could one day be.

OPPOSITE *Covered head-to-toe in blood, scales, herring sperm, and roe, crewman Justin Pleier shows how messy commercial fishing can be.* RIGHT *Crewmen reload a gill net after bringing in a haul of herring.*

LEFT *The sun rises over Kulukak Bay as the skipper and crew of the F/V Megan Dee get ready for the next round of herring fishing.*

ABOVE *The hectic life of commercial fishing presents rare opportunities to rest.*

AFTER MORE THAN 50 YEARS in the commercial fishing industry, Violet Willson could easily remember how she started as a winter watchman at the old Bumblebee Cannery in South Naknek. She had married Guy Groat, Jr. and lived on the Branch River before her time in the cannery. Later, her family moved across the river to Naknek. Violet raised her family on fishing, earning a living as a commercial fisherman for fifty-one years, working for Ocean Beauty for the last twenty years of her career and bringing in additional fish to feed the family through a subsistence lifestyle. The fisheries gave her family "a very good life," Violet says. "All of my children and grandchildren are involved in fishing today."

A FISHING FAMILY

One of Violet's granddaughters, Carmill, was "teethed on salmon jerky." As far back as she can remember, Carmill was part of the fishing life. Her husband, LouDell, worked on two set net sites in Naknek, at the mouth of the river, that belong to other family members. Rhonda, another of Violet's granddaughters, started fishing on the bay's west side, the Kvichak side, when she was just seven years old; she fished there until she was fifteen. Rhonda, her husband, and their son now work two set net sites in the summer, contributing some of their catch to Ocean Beauty and some to Naknek Family Fisheries, where Rhonda, her brother, and their mother are investors.

Rhonda's brother, Everett, is a drift boat captain. The skipper of the *Chulyen* (an Athabascan word for "raven"), he has been fishing since he was seven years old, when he spent his first season on a drift boat. He had a set net permit in his name by age eleven, ran his own set net operation as a teenager, and owned his own drift net permit by twenty-one. Working early in the fishing industry allowed Everett to pay for his own braces, four-wheelers, and other needs and amenities while growing up in Naknek.

Everett's sister Izetta, the mastermind behind Naknek Family Fisheries, founded the company in 2006 and began processing a year later. She and her husband, Chet, work side by side processing and preparing orders. Exposure to her grandmother's work as a fisherman and at the cannery motivated Izetta to develop an independent processor. Her vision for the family fishery is to provide an alternative to the large processors for area fisherman. Growing up, Izetta noticed that fishermen treated the fish for the Groat family better than what they sent to the commercial processors—she wanted to preserve that sense of quality. While the Groat family is not unusual in the Naknek community in that fishing is part of life, it is certainly extraordinary in the breadth and depth of its involvement in fishing: four generations of fisherman, a drift boat captain, set net operators, and a family processing facility. ∼

OPPOSITE *Violet Willson at her home in Naknek, surrounded by generations of family photos*
ABOVE *The tender* Westward *ties up next to the barge* Bristol Lady *in Egegik Bay to exchange supplies.*

ABOVE *Bags of gill nets sit on the Ocean Beauty dock in Naknek, waiting to be loaded onto a tender for delivery to fishing boats out in Bristol Bay.*
BELOW *Rhonda and her son prepare to deliver their evening's catch to the beach tender for delivery to Naknek Family Fisheries.*

ABOVE *Sockeye salmon sit on ice in totes on the beach in Naknek, waiting delivery to Naknek Family Fisheries.*

ABOVE *Paul Wayner, Rhonda's husband, drives their set net boat back to the beach in Naknek to deliver their catch.*
BELOW *A tender and barge are anchored out in Ugashik Bay.*

LEFT *"Picking" fish from a gill net is tedious and slimy work.*

TOP *Totes full of iced Sockeye salmon await delivery to various canneries in Naknek.*

ABOVE *After being caught, Sockeye salmon are stowed in a chilled hold in the fishing boat to await delivery to a tender.*

LEFT *Drift boats come in to the mouth of the Ugashik River to deliver their catch to a waiting tender.*

RIGHT *A full moon rises above the gill net onboard the F/V N20 as the boat and crew wait for the next commercial fishing opener in Naknek.*

ABOVE *The drum spins as a crew member of the F/V Curragh lets out the net near "the line" at Naknek.*

LEFT *The crew and skipper of the F/V Chulyen pick fish from a gill net.*
RIGHT *A pair of Sockeye salmon cling to a gill net as the crew starts to haul in the catch.*

ABOVE *The crew of the F/V Megan Dee works late into the night to haul in herring in Kulukak Bay.*

RIGHT *The sun rises and it is another beautiful day for commercial fishing.*

OPPOSITE *Floating pro-cessing facilities receive and package herring near the village of Togiak.*
RIGHT *The skipper and crew of the F/V Megan Dee deliver a catch of her-ring to an anchored tender in Kulukak Bay.*

ABOVE *An Ocean Beauty truck delivers wild Alaskan Sockeye salmon to the fish-mongers at Pike Place Market in downtown Seattle.*

RIGHT *Commercial fishing drift boats wait at the Dillingham harbor for the next Sockeye opener.*

Everett Thompson

Everett flies a "No Pebble" flag from his boat, the F/V Chulyen, *and regularly provides information and materials to other commercial fishing operators about the Pebble Mine.*

Recognizable because of its "No Pebble" flag hanging from the main mast, it is easy to see the *F/V Chulyen* on approach. Its skipper, Everett Thompson, carries extra "No Pebble" stickers on board and is always ready to talk about the Pebble development. When he first learned of the Pebble exploration and the planned mine development, he was open-minded about it, and set out to learn more. But after he learned about the development plans and the impacts of mining, he became increasingly opposed to it. Behind that opposition was a strong family connection to the resource. He has an incredible knowledge of his family history and that of the region, both of which are steeped in the world of commercial fishing. His family traditions combine the commercial and subsistence side of fishing, as well as the commercial catching and processing of fish. Year after year, he seems to have an innate sense as to where the fish will be and when, and he knows where to intercept the fish as they come in to follow their instinctive path up the river systems. He also is proficient at "toeing the line," making sure he stays in legal compliance as a fisherman. He knows the area so well, that he even fished every district in a single year—a feat he is not aware of any other boat accomplishing. ⁓

OPPOSITE *A commercial fishing drift boat rests on the mud during low tide on the Naknek River, while the Old Bumblebee Cannery in South Naknek basks in evening light.*

Nick Jans

AN EMBARRASSMENT OF RICHES

Photographer Carl Johnson leans into his Nikon. Twenty feet away, a lone gray wolf stands, surveying the tidal flat before him as if our small group did not exist. The wolf trots on with scarcely a glance our way. Minutes later, without moving, we share a frame-filling encounter with a huge, fight-scarred male brown bear, so close that our guide, Dustin, has to take action. A calm wave of arms, a firm *Hey, bear,* and the eight-hundred-pound behemoth deflects past us and continues grazing on succulent sedges a few dozen paces away. With so much forage available, and decades of peaceable interaction, these resident bears tend to see humans as neither food source nor threat. We have become part of the landscape.

A lone wolf stares curiously at a group of photographers in Katmai National Park and Preserve.

Not once but many times over our four-day stay, Carl turns to me, grins, and shakes his head at the incredible opportunities that pass before us—from an eagle nest with chicks viewed from above to a fox teasing a young bear to a seal nursery and rafts of sea otters. And so many brown bears we can scarcely count them: foraging, playing, swimming, courting, mothers nursing cubs. The experience resounds beyond photography. We roam beaches with fossils and artifacts at our feet; glide past rocky pinnacles where clouds of nesting seabirds wheel; drift among feeding humpback whales; catch rod-bending halibut and cod; become filled with the whir of wind and water, and the land's deep silence beyond.

We are guests at Katmai Wilderness Lodge on the outer coast of Katmai National Park and Preserve, on the southeastern edge of the Bristol Bay region. Though by itself, Katmai is immense—nearly five million wilderness acres, including a spectacularly ragged, unpeopled 497-mile coast—it is a fraction of the almost unimaginable sweep of the expanse. All that

Carl and I have seen are mere tokens of the riches and variety that Bristol Bay offers the recreational visitor: volcanic moonscapes; enormous freshwater lakes and sprawling river systems; high tundra, rolling forests, and vast wetlands; spectacular, glacier-draped mountain ranges; pristine, current-swirled ocean waters, fjords, and tidal flats—all of them brimming with life. This fertile merging of land and sea spills toward a seemingly limitless horizon, one valley and one bay to the next, each unique yet part of a larger untrammeled whole.

A thirty-six-year resident of Alaska, I have traveled tens of thousands of wilderness miles in some of the state's most remote and scenic landscapes—from the austere enormity of the Brooks Range to the fjord-incised rain forests of Southeast Alaska. I have frequently nudged outdoors-oriented visitors toward the Bristol Bay area as a remote yet accessible distillation of the best that wild Alaska has to offer. The sheer volume and variety of protected wilderness areas bespeaks the region's status as a world-class natural reserve. These include Lake Clark and Katmai National Park and Preserve; Togiak, Alaska Maritime, Alaska Peninsula/Becharof, and Izembek National Wildlife refuges; the Wood Tikchik State Park and McNeil River State Game Sanctuary and Preserve—all told, a staggering twenty-four-million-plus acres combined. Wildlife viewing and photography; wilderness backpacking and float trips; bird watching; sport fishing and hunting; mountaineering, flightseeing and coastal cruising or kayaking—Bristol Bay offers a kaleidoscope of recreational possibilities.

Neither planning a trip, nor the actual getting to Bristol Bay are nearly as daunting as one might suppose. Dozens of quality lodges, guides, flying services, and outfitters are poised online to answer questions or help you custom-craft your dream trip. Travel between

LEFT *A guide from the Katmai Wilderness Lodge and a group of clients observe a brown bear boar grazing along a river.*
OPPOSITE *A pair of hikers look out over Twin Lakes in Lake Clark National Park and Preserve.*

modern airports, to within a jumping-off distance of your chosen destination, is no more complicated than in the Lower 48. The final flight in, typically less than an hour, usually in a pontoon-equipped float plane landing on a lake or river, is an integral part of the journey, offering stunning bird's-eye perspectives and a fitting transition into another world. The wild country scrolls below like a living map, then draws closer and closer as the plane noses downward and the floats make rushing contact with the water, signaling your arrival.

The keystone of Bristol Bay's wealth can be summed up in one word: salmon. Thousands of waterways, from pouring, rapid-studded rivers to ankle-deep creeks, surge with overlapping runs of one, or all five Pacific species, great tide-like pulses that drive the region's ecology and economy. They boil inland, providing a conveyor belt of energy from ocean to far inland that lasts from summer's lush greens into the snows of late autumn. A profusion of lakes provide vital nurseries for millions of juvenile salmon as well as habitat for other fish and wildlife. Alaska's iconic brown bears and moose as well as tiny warblers benefit from the massive infusion of sea-grown biomass. Analysis of practically every living thing, including plant life, shows signature chemical traces of energy that came from salmon. Without their gifts, the land simply would not be what it is.

The value of recreational tourism, much of it tied directly or indirectly to salmon, amounts to well over $100 million annually—a staggering sum, given the region's modest population. The sport-hunting industry accounts for an estimated $12 million; wildlife viewing and other nonconsumptive tourism, $17 million. Sport fishing, mostly in freshwater, is calculated to be worth more than $60 million—a prodigious

renewable resource on which many livelihoods depend, both within the region and far beyond. Dozens of lodges and outfitting services offer access to these riches in a land where the water is indeed gold.

Those who make their living from the land by sharing with others intend to keep it that way. "There's a super high interest in adventure-based tourism," says David Coray, owner of Silver Salmon Creek Lodge, a private inholding in Lake Clark National Park and Preserve [David is the brother of Anne Coray, who co-wrote the essay "Moving with the Seasons" in this book]. A life-long resident of the region, he says, "Our focus is a sustainable model with minimal impact on the land. We're stewards and educators. . . . We want to be agents of change for future preservation efforts, and to carry that battle forward."

A brown bear boar looks down at spawning Sockeye salmon in a small creek near Iliamna Lake.

A boat of lodge guests observe a humpback whale surface in Kukak Bay of Katmai National Park and Preserve.

If salmon are the land's lifeblood, the waterways are its veins. Rivers with musical names twine across the land: Mulchatna, Kanektok, Aniakchak, Koktuli, Naknek, Goodnews, Kvichak, and more stretch over the horizon, enough to require not one but several lifetimes to know. Rising behind the salmon, trout, char, and grayling grow huge, gorging on dislodged eggs and the husks of the spawned-out salmon. In some situations three well-placed casts with either fly or spinning tackle might land as many different species. Often, the main difficulty is not coaxing fish to strike but getting past smaller individuals or less-desired species. Trophy catch-and-release fly fishing for rainbow trout in remote streams is a marquee draw—robust, deep-bodied fish commonly exceeding two feet in length,

with much larger specimens possible on any given cast. Deep, glacier-incised lakes such as hundred-mile-long Iliamna and mountain-framed, postcard-scenic Lake Clark hold not only rainbows and char but outsized lake trout and pike. In fact, the Bristol Bay area cradles four of Alaska's five largest lakes and hundreds of smaller ones, the vast majority of them worth at least a few casts.

For nonfishers the region's vast, varied, and scenic melding of water and land lends itself to wilderness journeys. Backcountry trips combining river and lake travel, hiking, photography, and fishing can be custom-shaped to a wide range of abilities, interests, trip lengths, and comfort levels. In the course of photographing this book, Carl Johnson faced the

not-so-onerous task of sampling a few options. Besides our shared experience at Katmai Wilderness Lodge, he spent several days at Silver Salmon Creek Lodge, which also specializes in bear and nature photography with all the comforts of home. He traveled to No See Um Lodge, owned by John Holman, a leader of the fight against the Pebble Mine. This latter establishment has long provided no-compromises, personalized fly-fishing experiences for discerning anglers from around the world. Carl also joined a five-day guided kayak trip with Alaska Alpine Adventures, paddling and hiking in the heartbreakingly gorgeous Twin Lakes area of Lake Clark National Park and Preserve. "Paddling is my preferred method of travel," he says. "My inspiration for being a nature photographer was born during two years working as a canoe guide. . . . [Paddling] provides an ongoing opportunity for exploring new photographic subjects, new compositions."

No matter the reason for visiting the Bristol Bay region, the experience will amount to far more than the sum of its parts—not just a trout or salmon glistening like a living jewel in your hands; or a mountain peak awash in alpenglow, mirrored in a transparent lake; or a group of bears foraging in a mist-shrouded tidal flat. Guests of this place emerge with a sense of connection to a larger whole—a vast, complex world whose beauty is defined by its unbounded scale. There are no highways, no large-scale industrial development just over the horizon. Bristol Bay resonates in the collective imagination, cradling the intrinsic value of the unseen.

Inevitably your stay ends. The process of arriving reverses as the plane roars and lifts free; the country you have brushed against fades and that busy other world resumes. The experience, though, echoes through your being. If the Bristol Bay region remains protected and intact, it will be because we willed it so. ⌇

LEFT *Chef Julius Rhymes prepares to serve a meal of fresh-caught salmon to guests at the Silver Salmon Creek Lodge.*
OPPOSITE *A skiff rests on the shore of the Kvichak River near the No See Um Lodge.*

ABOVE *A trio of DeHavilland Beavers rests for the night before another busy day of ferrying sport fishing clients at the No See Um Lodge on the Kvichak River.*
RIGHT *A meandering stream near the Kvichak River*

TRIP
OF A
LIFETIME

IN 1968, DICK PROENNEKE CHOSE TO RETIRE by moving to the shores of Twin Lakes in the Lake Clark region of Alaska and building a log cabin by hand from materials on the land. As time moved on, the land around him became federally designated wilderness and incorporated into a new national park. As a result, his cabin and the land he loved are now prime destinations for backcountry travelers.

It was the reputation of the region that brought a motley gathering together in the hot summer of 2013: a pair of carpenters from New Jersey, a Malaysian couple from Singapore, a retired couple from Arizona, a young woman preparing to enter the US Coast Guard Academy, and the owner of a global health and nonprofit consulting firm in Seattle. The great appeal for the visitors was the combination of paddling and hiking, the opportunity to explore the "real" outdoors, the chance to visit a historic cabin, and the allure of wildness that Alaska offers. After gathering together and consolidating gear at Port Alsworth, the visitors and their guides began the process of ferrying gear and people out to the drop-off in Lower Twin Lakes. This process required each of two Cessna 286 aircraft, operated by Lake Clark Air, to make four round trips. Over the next six days in the backcountry, the group would base camp, day hike to the top of nearby peaks, paddle the turquoise waters of Twin Lakes, line their inflatable kayaks between the two lakes, and visit the Proenneke cabin site.

As for the travelers, each took away something different from the trip. For Mo, the Coast Guard cadet, it was "mind-blowing" to be in Alaska and hiking to the top of a peak to view the expansive scenery. For Mike, one of the carpenters, the vastness and beauty of the area was hard for him to articulate. As for Stan, the other carpenter, although his primary motivation was to see the Proenneke cabin, he was impressed with Alaska's immense wilderness and how small it made him feel. For Melissa, the consulting firm owner, being away from technology and learning about the land was most beneficial. For Ray and Anna Marie, the retirees, who had already made several trips to Alaska, kayaking in one of the wilder parts of Alaska was on their bucket list. But Derrick and Christine of Singapore had a different take. Christine was amazed by the sunsets and tundra, but she decided that she would tell people to stay away from Lake Clark: "I want to have it all to myself. I don't want anyone to come to Lake Clark. This is so beautiful—it is just beyond comprehension." ⌒

ABOVE *A pair of inflatable kayaks rests on the shore of Lower Twin Lake.*

OPPOSITE *Christine and Derrick Jong of Singapore launch their kayak during a Twin Lakes trip in the Lake Clark backcountry.*
ABOVE *Alaska Alpine Adventures guide Nick Allen changes into dry shoes after being dropped off with the week's supplies.*

BELOW *Tent and evening light on the Chigmit Mountains near Twin Lakes*
RIGHT *Cloudy skies and winds at Upper Twin Lake*

A fly fisher tries his luck during low tide at Silver Salmon Creek.

RIGHT, TOP *Rainbow trout on a hook while still in the crystal-clear waters of a stream near Iliamna Lake.* BOTTOM *Fishing for rainbow trout, which is a highly sought sport fishing species, is catch-and-release-only in most parts of Bristol Bay.*

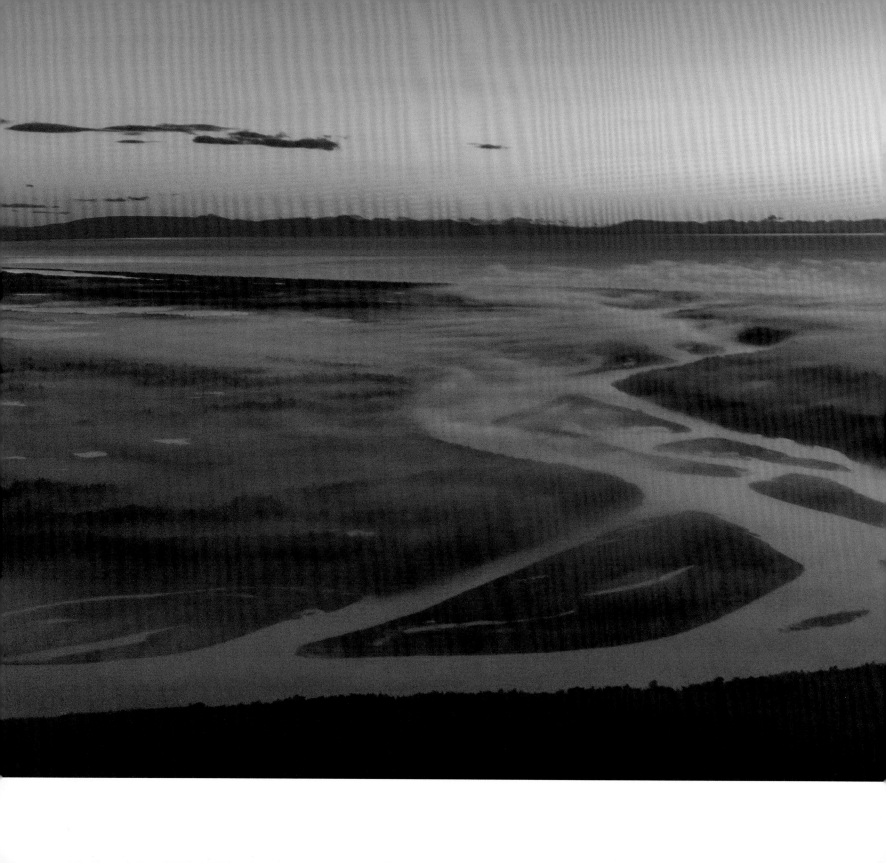

LEFT *The colors of dawn light up the sky over a foggy Kvichak River.*
ABOVE *Morning light catches cabins at the No See Um Lodge on the Kvichak River.*

ABOVE *A group of guided lodge guests photograph a brown bear sow and her two cubs in Lake Clark National Park and Preserve.*
OPPOSITE *Brown bear cubs sparring*

LEFT, TOP *Interior view of Dick Proenneke's cabin, built solely with hand tools and from local materials, in the wilderness of Lake Clark National Park and Preserve.*
BOTTOM *Stan Romanek of New Jersey looks through the open upper door of the cabin on Twin Lakes.*
OPPOSITE *Exterior view of the stone chimney*

LEFT *Blue phlox decorates the shore of Lower Twin Lake at sunset.*
ABOVE *A tufted puffin flies along the surface of the water in Hallo Bay of Katmai National Park and Preserve.*

LEFT *A brown bear sow stolls away from the mouth of Silver Salmon Creek with a Coho (silver) salmon—the first catch of the season.*

OPPOSITE *Silver Salmon Creek Lodge guests hike out during incoming tide for a boat trip to nearby Chisik Island where they'll view puffins.*

Erin McKittrick

TREASURES IN THE LAND

Ankle-high tundra plants thrummed in a wind that set their berries dancing. Cold rain slapped my coat. A helicopter thundered overhead. I palmed a handful of cranberries, then stepped back to where my blackened titanium pot bubbled on a fire of willow twigs in the heart of the largest mineral prospect in North America. Named for its resemblance to the green expanse of the Pebble Beach golf course in California, the Pebble Mine prospect is a remote slice of tundra in a more remote corner of Alaska, upstream of Bristol Bay. Far from the cruise lines and highways, this is a land of shimmering lakes and rolling hills, of clear creeks lined by willows and moose, of wetlands and birdsong and the punishing wind that rushes between the Bering Sea and Cook Inlet.

Aerial view of rolling hills and ponds near the Pebble Mine exploration.

139

More than that, it is a land of salmon. Only 7500 people live in the Bristol Bay watershed, an area of some 46,000 square miles. But there are *millions* of fish here. Its glacier-carved lakes and spring-fed streams are the perfect rearing habitat for the tens of millions of salmon that return to the bay each year. Bristol Bay has the largest Sockeye run in the world, and all five species of Pacific salmon swim here in abundance—with no dams, no hatcheries, nothing but wild winding rivers to meet the returning throngs. The water flowing from this spot—this would-be mine— can touch half of them, the ten million Sockeye salmon that return each year to the Nushagak and Kvichak River basins.

Mining the Alaskan wilderness is nothing new. As soon as the first outsiders landed on Alaska's shores, they sought to dig beneath them. For the coal that crumbled from the bluffs. The oil bubbling out of beach sands. The gold nuggets glinting in the creeks. America's first Alaskan story was that of the Klondike Gold Rush, where grizzled prospectors fanned out across the territory, hunched under backbreaking loads, with picks and shovels and bags of flour and optimistic dreams about what might be beyond

ABOVE *Excavated land-scape above the closed Berkeley Pit in Butte, Montana.*

RIGHT *The Berkeley Pit remains full of toxic water long after it was closed in 1982. It remains today one of many active Superfund sites in the area.*

the next mountain. The romance of mining was the romance of independent self-sufficiency. Toughness and entrepreneurial spirit and adventure. It bore more resemblance to my twenty-first-century backpacking trip than to the mining enterprise that occupied the valley today. At the Pebble Mine prospect, drill rigs pierced four thousand feet beneath the berries and reindeer moss, slurping nearly three hundred gallons of fuel each day they pushed deeper. Helicopters passed by constantly in their missions of resupply. By 2011 they had needled this spot with more than a thousand holes. The ultimate plan was to remove the valley entirely. The open pit would reach down farther into the valley floor than the three-thousand-foot mountains that rise above it, creating one of the largest open pit mines on the continent. Tunnels would snake out from the bottom of the pit, seeking out deeper ore, collapsing and consuming the mountains above them. Great earthen walls would reach 750 feet above the valley floor, damming off an eight-square-mile lake of toxic mine tailings. Those tailings—up to 10.7 billion tons of pulverized rock—would be a thousand times heavier than the Great Pyramid of Egypt. If you piled them into a pyramid shape, they would form a mountain far larger than any real peak in the region: a conical monstrosity over seven thousand feet tall.

The reason for this mind-boggling scale is the same reason the prospectors trudged right past the fifty-eight billion pounds of copper, molybdenum, and gold here. The metals are present only deep beneath the surface, and only in vanishingly small concentrations. If the Pebble deposit were an apple pie, the edible part would amount to less than a teaspoon. The copper here is only 0.34 percent of the ore. Molybdenum is 0.023 percent. Gold only 0.00003 percent, or 0.01 ounces in a ton. With modern technology, we can find that teaspoon. We truly can extract the needle from the haystack. The problem is what happens to the rest of it.

Nearly ninety million years ago, the earth boiled here. Deep below the surface, magma-heated water flowed up through fractured rocks. Metals dissolved in those blistering streams, then precipitated in cracks and pockets near the surface, bound to sulfur. These ores are not the shining pure flakes picked up by prospectors. These ores are a chemical reaction waiting to happen. The earth provides the water and oxygen. The mine provides the rock. Together they are a recipe for toxic waste. Specifically, they are a recipe for turning the metal sulfides in the ore into sulfuric acid. A mining company will tell you, correctly, that nearly all its "toxic waste" is just plain old rock. Plain old rock, shattered by dynamite and pulverized into flour, millions of times faster than it could have eroded naturally. Mine tailings multiply the surface area, until every single side of every single speck is exposed to oxygen. The reaction that was imperceptibly slow beneath a mountain is now furiously fast—test tube chemistry at a landscape scale.

The only way to prevent it is to keep the rock from air. Mining engineers design enormous artificial lakes to bury their waste. They build water treatment plants to control the leaks and seeps that spring out around them. But acid still flows from mines dug by the Romans, just as it plagues our most modern

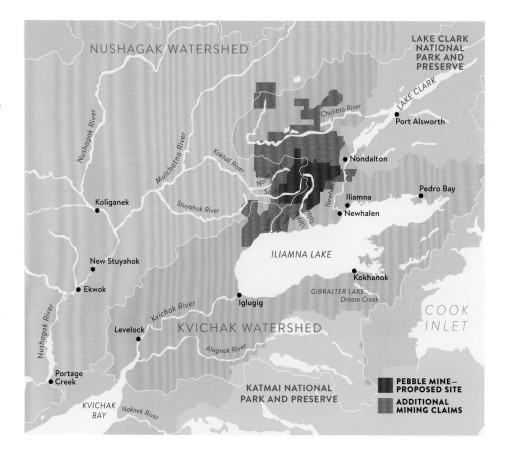

constructions. This is acid mine drainage. In some mines the water can become a thousand times more acidic than battery acid. At many mines, nearby creeks become so caustic that only "extremophile" microbes can survive. Metals—including arsenic, lead, and copper—dissolve more easily in acid. Those metals continue downstream, where even the smallest concentrations can wreak havoc.

At a few parts per billion—equivalent to a few seconds in a hundred years—copper can render salmon and trout more vulnerable to infection. It can impair their sense of smell that allows them to navigate to the streams of their birth and avoid predators. It can kill

Pebble Prospect is only one of several mining claims in the Kvichak and Nushagak watersheds. If the Pebble Mine were developed, other mines would likely follow, turning prime salmon habitat into a massive industrial area.

Rick Halford stands by one of his planes at his family's home near Lake Alegnagik.

some plankton species at the base of the food chain. In higher concentrations—dozens of parts per billion—copper can kill fish outright. What harms the streams affects the entire ecosystem. Bears eat salmon. Moose eat aquatic plants. Migratory birds and tiny wood frogs eat the insects that incubate in the pools and streams. Fish and birds do not submit comments to federal agencies or put protest stickers on the bumpers of their cars. But Bristol Bay is full of more than just salmon. It is full of salmon people. There are eight Alaska Native villages downstream of the Pebble Mine site, and five more nearby. There are twelve thousand people netting and processing fish in Bristol Bay each summer. Sport fishermen fly in from thousands of miles away to catch a trophy rainbow trout.

The Pebble deposit was discovered in 1988. And for the next decade and a half, it was explored, set aside, explored, sold and purchased, and quietly explored again—all under the radar of pretty much everyone. This is not surprising. In a slice of five years time, metal mining exploration might occur at nearly one hundred unknown prospects across Alaska, half of which will be abandoned nearly as soon as they are begun. Pebble was different. In 2004 a Canadian exploration company, Northern Dynasty Minerals, more than doubled its estimate of metals in the ground and announced that its exploration efforts would move to development.

Immediately Pebble's neighbors were skeptical. Opposition to the project began in one-room village community centers, next to the pile of bingo boards, over paper plates of moose and akutaq (Eskimo ice cream). In rubber boots and raingear on the deck of a drift boat. Under the giant trout mounted on the shining wood wall of an upscale lodge. One of these neighbors proved to be an important but unlikely ally—ultraconservative multimillionaire Bob Gillam—sport fisherman, owner of a wilderness home in the area, and principal funder of the Pebble opposition campaign, to the tune of $3 million per year. In the first few years more than ten local village councils and tribes had passed resolutions opposing Pebble, joined by a variety of Alaskan environmental groups, as well as the Alaskan Inter-Tribal Council, the Alaska Independent Fishermen's Marketing Association, and the Alaska Wilderness Recreation and Tourism Association. The coalition opposing the project was nonpartisan (Alaska's prominent Republican senator, the late Ted Stevens, was an opponent, along with some Republican ex-governors) and primarily local. The opposed villages formed their own organization: Nunamta Aulukestai, Caretakers of Our Land. Bristol Bay fishing boats flew "No Pebble Mine" flags. Bumper stickers—"Pebble Mine" circled and slashed in red—could be seen around the state. Outside of Alaska, however, almost no one had heard of it yet.

In 2007 the tiny Northern Dynasty Minerals company partnered with Anglo American, a giant multinational mining corporation. The next year, $140 million flowed into the Pebble prospect. Some of that created

CLOCKWISE FROM TOP LEFT *Aerial view of six sump pits, designed to collect waste material from drilling material, at a Pebble Mine exploration site / Waste sump pits / Plugged borehole and remediated exploration site / In-use drilling rig and sump pits (Photos courtesy Rick Halford)*

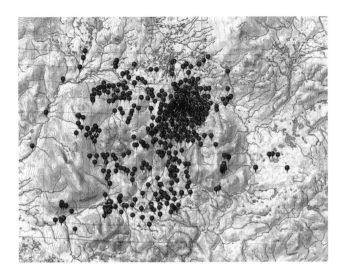

Geographic Information System (GIS) plotting of 1269 boreholes drilled during over 25 years of the Pebble Prospect exploration, at the headwaters of the South Fork Koktuli River and Upper Talarik Creek, which flows into Iliamna Lake. (GIS graphic courtesy of Stu Smith)

150,000 feet of new drill holes. $14 million of it went right to public relations. A Google news search for Pebble Mine brings up just one hit from 2005. By 2011 there were sixteen pages of results. Pebble had become the most controversial issue in the state, and its infamy had spread around the world. Jewelers pledged not to use gold from Pebble, should any ever be produced. Seafood chefs spoke out against it. Local activists took jets halfway around the world to speak before Anglo American shareholders, while outsiders buzzed over the now-famous Pebble site in Alaska senator Rick Halford's prop plane. Documentaries played around the country. The "No Pebble" bumper stickers could be seen in Seattle. And through all of it, the locals—Native people and fishermen—continued to speak, their voices amplified by the infusion of outside money, and echoed by people who had never set foot in Bristol Bay.

Perhaps it is because salmon have been so beleaguered in most of their former strongholds that they are clung to so firmly in Bristol Bay. California, Oregon, and Washington have less than 10 percent of the wild salmon they once did. A 2011 report from Washington state estimated the costs of habitat recovery plans there at over $500 million per year. Similar efforts occur across much of the Pacific salmon's range, attempting to restore dwindled and endangered runs to some semblance of their former glory. Bristol Bay is different. Here salmon runs are still what they once were everywhere, with all the vibrant resilience that comes from wild stocks, large populations, and rich genetic diversity.

The Pebble deposit is on Alaska state land, but the state government is not the only agency with authority here. Under section 404(c) of the Clean Water Act, the Environmental Protection Agency (EPA) can prohibit filling or dredging of wetlands, lakes, or streams—effectively preventing mining—if it would have unacceptable adverse effects. In 2013 the EPA's draft watershed announcement showed unacceptable negative impacts. In 2014 the final assessment was released, and the agency announced its plan to invoke its authority to protect Bristol Bay. The Pebble Partnership launched a lawsuit in response. Between the time of the EPA's initial announcement and the Pebble Partnerships lawsuit, two large investors (Anglo American and Rio Tinto) pulled out. Metal prices dropped. The company's stock tanked. The Pebble prospect had become a series of legal challenges winding their long way through the courts. The lull in Pebble's story lets us breathe and zoom out. The land around the Pebble deposit is not a protected area. It is still a mining claim, surrounded by other mining claims, which cover half a million acres in the region on state, federal, and Native corporation lands. It took water and time for glaciers to carve out this landscape. Water and time for the metals to precipitate deep beneath the earth. And if any mine is built here, water and time will eventually contaminate it. Over 90 percent of mines in a setting

of diversion trenches and pipes. Dams and pumps and settling tanks. Digital readouts and whirring generators. Pyramid-like stacks of shipping containers full of neutralizing lime. This is Red Dog Mine, where each and every year seven workers will take $10 million to ship in 7300 tons of lime to turn 1.4 billion gallons of toxic water into seventy thousand tons of sludge and then find somewhere to put it. Forever. It's utterly impossible. Some year, some decade, some century, that plan will fail. Every sulfide mine has a plan just like that tucked into a folder somewhere. We let them do it. We always have, across all the Superfund sites and acidic rivers that speckle the American West. Once unearthed, mine tailings never become safe again. Tailings are forever. No matter what happens at the Pebble deposit, acid mine drainage will continue to be an issue—across Alaska, across the nation, and across the world—unless we change our federal laws. What if mines were only allowed to build what they could walk away from? To leave behind a site that required no perpetual maintenance, no perpetual employees, and no perpetual water treatment?

Bristol Bay is an ecosystem both exceptionally rich and exceptionally vulnerable. Its salmon are teeming. Its acid-generating potential is high, and its water runs everywhere in a complex and hard-to-catch hydrology. An active tectonic fault may even run beneath the mine site. But the biggest difference from other mine sites is that Bristol Bay has some exceptional human champions. Minerals—whether sequestered under the earth or ground up as mine tailings—are forever. But how long are we willing to watch over them? Because there are bright green valleys full of caribou, wetlands sparkling with mosquitoes, and rivers thick with the churning flow of Sockeye salmon. Here people live as part of this ecosystem, as tied to and dependent on the salmon as the bears are. Let that be our forever instead. ~

similar to the Pebble prospect (with acid-generating rock and nearby ground and surface water) polluted that nearby water, even over only a few decades.

Six hundred miles north of Pebble, there is a series

LEFT *A stream flows down to meet with Iliamna Lake.*
OPPOSITE *A young red fox runs past a brown bear boar in Kukak Bay.*

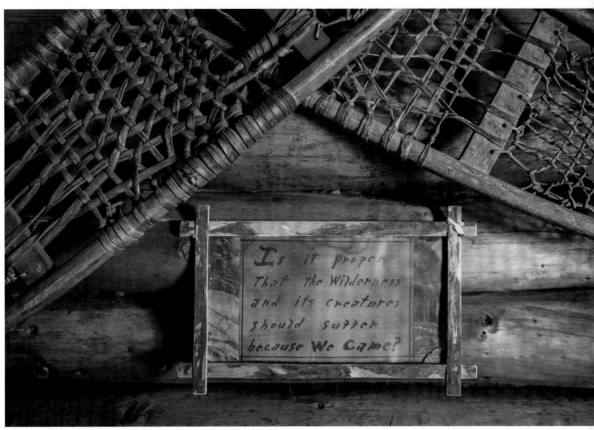

OPPOSITE *Iniskin Bay lies between Lake Clark and Katmai national parks, and is the planned site for the port facility that would be constructed to support the proposed Pebble Mine.*
ABOVE *Handwritten sign on the walls of Dick Proenneke's cabin in Lake Clark National Park and Preserve.*

Apayo Moore

Apayo is a Dillingham artist from a commercial fishing family who uses her talent to promote and advocate for a healthy salmon ecosystem in Bristol Bay.

A painting of a stream choked with Sockeye salmon at her Scaly Parts Gallery in Dillingham behind her, Apayo Moore exudes the same sense of playfulness and inspiration that permeates her work. With her nearly realistic portraits of salmon in the landscape, interpretive pieces about the life cycle of salmon, and whimsical "Salmon Love" series, after returning from Colorado with her Art Business degree Apayo quickly became a notable presence in the region. While in college, she was homesick and curious about what was happening back home. She started to focus on the Pebble development and learned about what hard rock mining would do to fish habitat. She grew up commercial fishing with her dad and does not remember ever not being on a boat in the summer. Bragging rights came in the form of who could pick fish the fastest. She was always connected to salmon and sympathetic to them, noting that she would throw back at least one salmon a season, "Just save one!" During college she spent her summers working at a fish counting tower for the Alaska Department of Fish and Game. Her sympathy for the plight of salmon took on steam when she returned home and became part of the "No Pebble" fight. Inspired by Ray Troll's work, she conceived the "Salmon Love" series about "two fish getting busy." ～

OPPOSITE *Tall grasses in a bluff overlooking the Nushagak River*

Lydia Olympic

*From the village of Igiugig
at the headwaters
of the Kvichak River,
Lydia fights to maintain a
rich cultural tradition.*

It is hard to imagine that someone from a remote village of sixty-nine people would be prepared to take on a multinational corporation. But that is what Lydia Olympic, from the village of Igiugig at the headwaters of the Kvichak River, set out to do. Like many people in the region, she grew up in fish camp, the annual tradition of staking out a spot on the river bank to harvest, cut, and smoke fish. One of the original "Pebble Warriors," Lydia was one of the early people in the region who took serious notice of what was happening away over the hills to the north, as hundreds of helicopter flights dramatically expanded the Pebble exploration. She learned about and visited hard rock mining sites, visited tribal leaders in areas that had been impacted by mining, and started to speak out against the development of the Pebble Mine. She was one of the select few who laid the foundation for what would become a strong, multi-pronged grassroots campaign to protect the Bristol Bay watershed. She took her passion into leadership positions, serving as her Tribal Council President and Vice-Chair of the National Tribal Operations Committee for the Environmental Protection Agency. Her fight is to maintain a rich cultural tradition. "Our traditional Native culture is already threatened and this mine would destroy our subsistence way of life and our spiritual connection to our land and waters. We must do all that we can to protect this extraordinary place with its unparalleled global resources." ≈

OPPOSITE *Frost and fog along the Kvichak River at the village of Igiugig.*

Monica Zappa, an Iditarod musher, gets some pre-race love from one of her teammates.

Monica Zappa races with her team down Fourth Avenue in Anchorage in her rookie year of the Iditarod and as part of her "Mushing to Save Bristol Bay" campaign.

CULINARY ACTIVISM: TWO CHEFS' PERSPECTIVES

WALKING INTO BLUEACRE SEAFOOD—an attractive, popular restaurant in downtown Seattle—the visitor's eye is drawn to the large marlin hanging on a back wall. Kevin Davis, owner and head chef of the restaurant, placed it there as a reminder of how species are impacted by overfishing pressures caused by demands in the restaurant industry. After all, he says, chefs are the "number one predator of the seafood world."

As a supporter of organizations that promote sustainable fisheries, like the Marine Stewardship Council and Long Live the Kings, Kevin accepts seafood only from the Pacific Northwest. That way, he knows the fisheries have been managed using the best available technology, in the most responsible way. This sustainable management compels him to include wild Alaska Sockeye salmon on Blueacre's menu. Kevin first heard about the Pebble prospect while watching the 2008 documentary *Red Gold*. Since then, he has become a culinary warrior in the effort to inform the public about the proposed Pebble Mine, often partnering with Trout Unlimited as part of its campaign to stop the mine's development. Several species of salmon are on the endangered species list in the Pacific Northwest, and Kevin hopes to be a part of preventing that from happening in Alaska.

Deep in the heart of the Nevada desert in Sin City, far from Alaska's salmon runs, Rick Moonen (head chef and owner of RM Seafoods at the Mandalay Bay Resort and Casino) calls his restaurant "seventeen thousand square feet of sustainability." His goal is to not to beat people over the head about sustainability; rather, he endeavors to show people that "we can be responsible, it can be delicious, and we can co-exist with our environment." He defines sustainability as making sure the restaurant industry does not take an active role in the extinction of any species. That means being part of efforts to avoid overfishing, bycatch, environmental destruction such as habitat loss, and the adverse impacts of aquaculture.

Sustainable seafood is crucial for feeding an exploding human population, Rick believes. This underscores the importance of preserving the viability of the Bristol Bay salmon fisheries. Already known as a recognized voice in sustainability, Rick has fought for genetically modified organism (GMO) labeling and has supported the "Give Swordfish a Break" campaign. He first learned about the Pebble prospect when he visited Cordova, Alaska, in connection with the bountiful Copper River Sockeye salmon runs. The more he learned about Pebble, the more he added his voice to the growing opposition. "The risks are too huge to justify the reward of bringing those metals to market," he says. ⌒

OPPOSITE *Copper River Sockeye salmon, the first large-scale commercial harvest of the season, is celebrated at Pike Place Market in Seattle.*
ABOVE *Chef Rick Moonen at his RM Seafood restaurant at Mandalay Bay in Las Vegas.*

LEFT *Wild Alaskan Sockeye salmon and a glass of pinot noir at the Blueacre Seafood restaurant.*
RIGHT *Chef Kevin Davis serves up wild Alaskan Sockeye salmon at his Blueacre Seafood restaurant in downtown Seattle.*

LEFT *The sun sets behind the Wood River Mountains and the Snake River within the Togiak National Wildlife Refuge.*

LEFT *Three glaciers converge in the heart of the Aleutian Range on the eastern edge of the Bristol Bay region.*
ABOVE *A traveler at the Pen Air counter in King Salmon wears a jacket expressing the sentiment of many.*

THE COST OF GOING BACK

IN THE LATE NINETEENTH CENTURY, Washington's Puget Sound was home to thriving ecosystems for several species of fish and a vibrant commercial fishing economy. Now, bocaccio, canary rockfish, Chinook salmon, and steelhead trout are on the NOAA Fisheries list of Endangered and Threatened Marine Species. Coho and Sockeye salmon are also listed as threatened or endangered in other portions of the Pacific Northwest. These declines in the region's fish populations were the result of death by a thousand cuts.

The US Army Corps of Engineers had its role, from clearing fallen logs (prime salmon habitat) to building levies. Railroads constructed tracks near major salmon habitat, building additional levies to support them. Approximately 70 percent of salt marsh habitat, critical to salmon rearing, was lost due to development. Riparian zones were heavily logged for decades. The construction of dams up and down the Pacific Northwest, starting with the first mainstem dam on the Columbia River in 1933, also contributed to steepening salmon population declines, some of which had been reduced by then to one-fifth of their pre-1850 numbers. Storm drains from the sprawling Seattle metropolis dump countless tons of waste into prime waterways.

Today, considerable effort and money has been directed at reversing damage and restoring salmon habitat. The collaborative effort of the Puget Sound Partnership involves tribes, state and federal agencies, and nonprofit organizations, with the goal of restoring Puget Sound ecosystems. According to a recent report from the Partnership, the cost of implementing freshwater restoration efforts is approximately $500 million; combating the effects of pollution is estimated at about $120 million.

The Stillaguamish Tribe operates a Chinook salmon hatchery. As Chinook salmon return to the North Fork of the Stillaguamish River, the Tribe captures sixty male and sixty female fish, spawns them, and then releases 250,000 hatchery juveniles every spring. This effort ultimately results in annual returns of 1000 to 1500 salmon for the past ten to fifteen years. The Tribe also returns logs to the river that the Army Corps of Engineers removed decades earlier. These combined efforts may restore habitat and populations in the North Fork.

Another broad-reaching effort targets dams. Removal of the four dams on the Snake River in Washington would mean converting from barge to rail delivery of products, increasing shipping costs $13 million a year, while replacing irrigation systems currently provided by the dams would cost another $421 million. In contrast, the estimated cost of salmon recovery without removing the dams ranges from $6 *billion* over the next ten years to $17 *billion* over the next twenty years—and salmon recovery without dam removal produces little result. ∼

OPPOSITE *Pat Stevenson, Environmental Manager for the Stillaquamish Tribe in Washington, shows some of the fallen logs the Tribe is working to place back in salmon streams as part of a habitat recovery effort.*

ABOVE *Radio host and writer Shannyn Moore speaks at a "No Pebble" event in Anchorage.*

LEFT *A popular sign in the Bristol Bay region.*

LEFT *Two exploratory drilling sites and an equipment staging area in the heart of the Pebble Mine Prospect.*

ABOVE *A spawned-out Sockeye salmon lies in the shallow bend of a creek near Iliamna Lake, marking the end of the lifecycle.*

LEFT *The South Fork of the Koktuli River starts its winding march down to the Metlakatla River, then Nushagak River and ultimately Bristol Bay.* OPPOSITE *Revelers get their funk on at the annual Salmonstock (now Salmonfest) event, a celebration of wild Bristol Bay salmon and a gathering of anti-Pebble Mine activists.*

ABOVE *A banner featuring art by Ray Troll is carried through a venue at Salmonstock.*

RIGHT *Ponds and lakes in the vicinity of the proposed Pebble Mine site demonstrate the interconnectedness and abundance of waterways in the area.*

OPPOSITE *Public art on the side of a building in Dillingham reflects local opinion about the proposed Pebble Mine.*
ABOVE *Former Alaskan First Lady Bella Hammond testifies in favor of the EPA's Bristol Bay Watershed Assessment at a hearing in Anchorage.*

ABOVE *A dragonfly rests on a board-walk railing near Brooks Falls in Kat-mai National Park and Preserve.*
RIGHT *Reeds and their reflection in the waters of a slough on the far north-eastern end of Lake Clark.*

ACKNOWLEDGMENTS

THE PHOTOGRAPHERS WHO INSPIRED me early in my career were also people who dedicated their talent to protecting and preserving wild places—photographers like Jim Brandenburg and Galen Rowell, and even the early greats like Ansel Adams and Elliot Porter. As I started to develop as a nature photographer, I followed their examples and donated, when I could, to local and national conservation groups that needed images for publications or fundraisers. When I met Robert Glenn Ketchum in 2005 at the 8th World Wilderness Congress, I purchased his book about the Alaskan Southwest, *Rivers of Life*. He inscribed my copy, "I hope this further inspires you to use your words and your photographs to further your conservation commitment." Well, Robert, I took that advice to heart and decided to devote my fulltime photographic attention to protecting Bristol Bay.

The five years of fieldwork that followed, the countless trips and absences from home would not have been possible without the steadfast love and support of my wife, Michelle.

I started with no funding support. The people and organizations that were pumping money into Bristol Bay were pretty tapped, and I knew I couldn't take out a second mortgage on our home—not if I wanted to keep Michelle's love and support. I needed to meet the right people. Happily, one of Michelle's coworkers, Valli Peterson, was from Naknek, the principal commercial fishing hub for the eastern side of Bristol Bay. She made arrangements for me to meet her family and spend time on the fishing boat of her cousin, Everett Thompson. Thus, my journey on this project was able to begin.

Valli's grandmother was Violet Willson, a respected elder and woman with over fifty years of experience in the commercial fishing industry. She was working as a winter watchman at the Old Bumblebee Cannery during the winter that delegates were debating the framework for the Alaska Constitution. I stayed in her home a few times during the life of this project, and she always made me feel welcome. I came to think of her as my Alaskan grandmother. Every time I visited, she sent me home with canned salmon. Unfortunately, she did not live to see the completion of this project.

Violet was my first introduction to the tremendous generosity of the people in this region, a mixture of Yup'ik, Aleut, Alutiiq, and Dena'ina Athabascan, as well as descendants of Swedish and Dutch immigrants drawn to the area to carry on fishing traditions. I cannot thank enough the people who hosted me and allowed me to come with them on hunting or fishing expeditions. Thanks to Everett Thompson and Rhonda Wayner for allowing me to spend time on their boats, as well as to Frank Woods III on the *F/V Megan Dee* and Daniel Blakey of the *F/V Curragh*, and to Dee Barker for taking me out on his set net boat on the Nushagak. There were also key commercial fishing contacts that helped to make things happen; thank you to Ocean Beauty Seafoods for allowing me to catch a ride on the tender *Westward* to meet up with the *F/V Chulyen*, and to Peter Pan Seafoods for a similar ride on a tender from the *F/V Megan Dee* in Kulukak Bay (to a floating processor where I caught a helicopter ride to the village of Togiak). Additionally, Izetta and Chet Chambers gave me access to their small family cannery, Naknek Family Fisheries.

Additional thanks to Bob Tracey of Nondalton for taking me out with him to check trap lines and for schooling me in the art of winter white fish harvesting using a jigger board. To Mark Dehmlow in Iliamna for hosting me and taking me out to harvest Sockeye. I must also give special note to Jack Hobson of Nondalton for taking me with him up the Chulitna River on his autumn moose hunt, for inviting me on the winter trail to visit his aunt and uncle, and for being my all-around ambassador to the village and region. Fish camp is a place that has deep family and generational roots, a place of warmth and sharing, of incredibly hard and tedious work, and I cannot thank enough those who welcomed me in to their fish camp: Natalia Marttila, Elizabeth Balluta, June Tracey, Tatiana Askoak, and Julianna Anelon.

Great kindness was shown to this stranger who randomly showed up on the beach, asking to photograph a family as they harvested Chinook and Sockeye from a subsistence set net: thank you, Monte and May Syvrud, for not only saying "yes" to my request but also inviting me to your home to learn how you cut fish (May scolding me for my poor technique) and hang it in your smoke house. Thank you also for insisting my nephew and I stay for dinner and join in a maqii (sweat) and for sending me home with a cooler full of salmon. All this for a stranger you had met on the beach. Sadly, Monte passed away in early 2015.

Another key contact in bringing pieces of this puzzle together was Melissa Blair of the National Parks Conservation Association who introduced me to Anne Coray and Steve Kahn and to Lydia Olympic in Igiugig. Melissa also opened the door at the Silver Salmon Creek Lodge.

I made a point to reach out to the Nondalton and Newhalen Tribal Councils before coming to the villages. They were very gracious and welcoming, and laid the groundwork for some key contacts. Although none of the images were used in the book, I would like to thank George Hornberger for taking me on a tour of the Tazimina Hydroelectric Plant to understand how the villages of Iliamna, Newhalen, and Nondalton were facing head-on the challenges of bringing less expensive power to rural Alaska.

Thanks especially to David and Joanne Coray of Silver Salmon Creek Lodge, Perry and Angela Mollan of Katmai Wilderness Lodge, John Holman of No See Um Lodge, and Dan Oberlatz of Alaska Alpine Adventures. Their support of this project was crucial in allowing me to capture key aspects of the recreational and tourism values of the region.

It would not have been possible to complete this project without the financial support of Amy Bachelor, Anchor Point Fund, National Parks Conservation Association, and Renewable Resources Foundation. Thank you to USA Artists and Hatchfund for providing the crowdfunding source that successfully funded most of the fieldwork. PEW provided invaluable funding at just the right time to make sure that the production of this book could continue. Special thanks also to Ground Truth Trekking for providing networking and organizational support early in the project. Thanks also to Timothy Hendricks for his volunteer service with Lighthawk that allowed me to capture many of the aerial images and to Lighthawk for its logistical support of pilots nationwide who seek to draw attention to issues of environmental concern. A heartfelt thank you to Rick Halford for additional aerial support in the vicinity of Dillingham. And thanks to BuzzBizz Studios for producing the fundraising video I used for crowd funding and for the initial design and production of the project website.

Thanks are due for the hard work of those at Braided River. For Helen Cherullo, who enthusiastically embraced my project and my vision, despite my not being a well-published photographer when I approached her. Crucial development in the text of this story would not have been possible without the fierce dedication of Deb Easter, who managed the writers and essays with such ease it seemed effortless. And I thank Mary Metz, project manager, for overseeing the work of designer Jane Jeszeck whose graphically compelling piece actually brought small tears to my eyes when I saw it for the first time.

Finally, I could not have successfully launched this project and pursued it without early, frequent and encouraging mentorship from Amy Gulick. I still don't think I have it all figured out, but thank you for getting me this far.

WITH APPRECIATION

THE MOUNTAINEERS FOUNDATION, a volunteer-run organization which supports the study, protection, and responsible enjoyment of the environment and natural areas, provided critical support for the publication of *Where Water is Gold*.

The Mountaineers Foundation proudly stewards, preserves, and restores the beautiful 386-acre Rhododendron Preserve on the Kitsap Peninsula in Washington State. Salmon and other wildlife abound in the Preserve. Much of the forest here has never been clearcut. At its heart lie nearly 70 acres of old-growth conifer forest, including one spectacular "Big Tree," a Douglas fir more than 30 feet in diameter. Stepping into the Preserve reminds one of what the Puget lowland looked like centuries ago, and what it could, through careful stewardship, look like again in centuries to come.

The Mountaineers Foundation has provided numerous grants for small-scale, short-term environmental projects covering a broad range of issues, from wildlife crossings to climate protection.

And, through their Paul Wiseman Conservation Education Grants, they support environmental projects which have significant educational benefits playing out over several years.

Their support for *Where Water is Gold* was given with the intention of giving residents of the Pacific Northwest the opportunity to learn more about the remarkable Bristol Bay region and to become personally invested in preserving the natural beauty and ecological integrity of this region, one whose health is so integrally interconnected with that of their own Salish Sea.

Visit http://mountaineersfoundation.org/ to learn more, or to support their work.

ABOUT THE PHOTOGRAPHER

JOSH MARTINEZ

CARL JOHNSON was born and raised in the Black Hills of South Dakota. He started his photography career while serving in the US Navy, where he was a ship's photographer for two commands and trained in a documentary and photojournalistic style. Early photographic successes included photographing the launch of a Tomahawk missile using a single-shot film camera. His later work as a canoe guide in the Boundary Waters Canoe Area Wilderness in northern Minnesota, along with his exposure to the writings of Sigurd Olson and the images of Jim Brandenburg, inspired his passion for nature photography. They also informed his belief in using photography to promote conservation.

Carl's greatest photographic passion lies in coming to fully understand a particular location, photographing all of its wonders, from small plants to vast landscapes, and increasingly the people who live with the land and call it home.

Carl has served as the artist-in-residence for Gates of the Arctic National Park and Preserve, Badlands National Park, and Rocky Mountain National Park. He was the "Environmental Issues" winner for the Windland Smith Rice International Awards in 2010 and earned two Honorable Mentions in the Wilderness Forever competition sponsored by *Nature's Best* magazine in 2014.

Carl lives in Anchorage, Alaska, with his wife, Michelle. You can view his photography on www.arcticlight-ak.com. You can also learn more about this project, the region, and its people at www.wherewaterisgold.com.

CONTRIBUTING WRITERS

CINDY DETROW

DAVE ATCHESON'S latest book is *Dead Reckoning: Navigating a Life on the Last Frontier, Courting Tragedy on Its High Seas* (Skyhorse Publishing), a memoir about his days as a commercial fisherman. He is also an avid fly fisher, teaches fly fishing at the University of Alaska, and is the author of the guidebook *Fishing Alaska's Kenai Peninsula* (Countryman Press) as well as National Geographic's *Hidden Alaska, Bristol Bay and Beyond*. He currently makes his home in Sterling, Alaska. For more information, see www.daveatcheson.com.

STEVE KAHN

ANNE CORAY is author of the poetry collections *Bone Strings* (Scarlet Tanager Books), *A Measure's Hush* (Boreal), and *Violet Transparent* (FutureCycle Press); coeditor of *Crosscurrents North: Alaskans on the Environment* (University of Alaska Press); and coauthor of *Lake Clark National Park and Preserve* (Alaska Geographic). A five-time Pushcart Prize nominee, Coray is the recipient of fellowships from both the Alaska State Council on the Arts and the Rasmuson Foundation. She lives at her birthplace on remote Lake Clark in Southwest Alaska.

NICK JANS

NICK JANS is a longtime contributing editor to *Alaska Magazine* and a member of *USA Today*'s board of editorial contributors. He has been published in a wide variety of magazines, from *Readers Digest* to *Rolling Stone*. He has also contributed to many anthologies and written eleven books. His latest two are *Once Upon Alaska* (a children's book with photographer Mark Kelley) and the national bestseller *A Wolf Called Romeo* (Houghton Mifflin). Upcoming projects include a just completed collection of essays and a long-simmering novel. A former resident of both the northwest Arctic and Juneau, Nick and his wife, Sherrie, now make their home in the Chilkat Valley north of Haines.

ANNE CORAY

STEVE KAHN is a lifelong Alaskan and a member of the Subsistence Resource Commission for Lake Clark National Park and Preserve. He lives a subsistence-based lifestyle with his wife, Anne Coray, on Lake Clark (Qizhjeh Vena) near the headwaters of the Bristol Bay watershed. He is author of *The Hard Way Home: Alaska Stories of Adventure, Friendship, and the Hunt* (University of Nebraska Press). He has published essays in *Alaska*, *ISLE*, and *Pilgrimage* and is a contributor to the anthologies *Wild Moments: Adventures with Animals of the North* and *Crosscurrents North: Alaskans on the Environment* (both published by University of Alaska Press). His nonfiction is drawn from years of wilderness experience from the Wrangell Mountains to the Bering Sea. Kahn and Coray coauthored *Lake Clark National Park and Preserve* (Alaska Geographic) and have won several writing awards as collaborators.

Born in Bridgeport, Connecticut, nature writer BILL SHERWONIT has called Alaska home since 1982. He has contributed essays and articles to a wide variety of newspapers, magazines, journals, and anthologies and is the author of more than a dozen books. His most recent books include *Animal Stories: Encounters with Alaska's Wildlife*; *Changing Paths: Travels and Meditations in Alaska's Arctic Wilderness*; and *Living with Wildness: An Alaskan Odyssey.*; Sherwonit's work primarily focuses on Alaska's wildlife and wildlands, but he's passionate about wild nature in all its varied forms, including the nature of his adopted hometown, Anchorage, and the spirited wildness we carry within us. *(Photo courtesy of Bill Sherwonit)*

SANDRA DAY O'CONNOR was the first woman to serve on the United States Supreme Court. She retired in 2006, after twenty-four years of service, to spend more time with her family. She received the Presidential Medal of Freedom in 2009. Justice O'Connor hosted a high-profile celebration of the natural bounty of America's Bristol Bay at the United States Supreme Court in Washington, DC, in 2011 that drew attention to the ecological, cultural, and economic value of the world-class salmon fisheries of the region. *(Photo collection of the Supreme Court of the United States)*

BRETWOOD HIGMAN

ERIN MCKITTRICK is a writer, adventurer, and scientist based in Seldovia, Alaska. When she's not there, Erin is most likely wandering across the wilderness with her husband and two children. She is the author of *A Long Trek Home: 4,000 Miles by Boot, Raft and Ski; Small Feet, Big Land: Adventure, Home and Family on the Edge of Alaska;* and *My Coyote Nose and Ptarmigan Toes: An Almost-True Alaskan Adventure.* You can find her at www .GroundTruthTrekking.org.

B R A I D E D   R I V E R

BRAIDED RIVER, the conservation imprint of Mountaineers Books, combines photography and writing to bring a fresh perspective to key environmental issues facing western North America's wildest places. Our books reach beyond the printed page as we take these distinctive voices and vision to a wider audience through lectures, exhibits, and multimedia events. Our goal is to build public support for wilderness preservation campaigns, and inspire public action. This work is made possible through the book sales and contributions made to Braided River, a 501(c)(3) nonprofit organization. Please visit BraidedRiver.org for more information on events, exhibits, speakers, and how to contribute to this work. Braided River books may be purchased for corporate, educational, or other promotional sales. For special discounts and information, contact our sales department at 800.553.4453 or mbooks@mountaineersbooks.org.

THE MOUNTAINEERS, founded in 1906, is a nonprofit outdoor activity and conservation organization, whose mission is "to explore, study, preserve, and enjoy the natural beauty of the outdoors . . . " Mountaineers Books supports this mission by publishing travel and natural history guides, instructional texts, and works on conservation and history.

Send or call for our catalog of more than 600 outdoor titles:
Mountaineers Books
1001 SW Klickitat Way, Suite 201
Seattle, WA 98134
800.553.4453
www.mountaineersbooks.org

Manufactured in China on FSC®-certified paper, using soy-based ink.

For more information, visit www.wherewaterisgold.com
© 2016 by Braided River
All rights reserved.
First edition, 2016
All essays ©2016 by the contributors
All essays on pages 38, 73, 74, 100, 113, 124, 150, 153, 156, and 160
© Carl Johnson
All photos © Carl Johnson unless credited otherwise
Photos on pages 36-37 © Pat Clayton

Cover photo: *Unnamed river delta in Kukak Bay, Katmai National Park and Preserve.* Frontispiece: *Golden light from a nearby bluff reflects with the green waters of Kulukak Bay.* Page 2: *The colors of autumn surround the braided Kvichak River.* Page 3: *A cow moose trots to shore after swimming from an island in Lake Clark.* Page 4: *A commercial fishing tender awaits the day's delivery after sunset.* Page 5: *Evening light catches a gill net being hauled into the bow of a drift boat.* Page 6: *Rick Delkittie, a resident of the village of Nondalton, looks out onto the frozen Sixmile Lake near his village.* Page 7: *An old wooden boat rests alongside the road in the village of Naknek.* Page 8: *A Dena'ina Athabascan elder sorts through cranberries for twigs and leaves.* Page 9: *A Bristol Bay snack of salmon strips, Sailor Boy Pilot Bread, and sugar for black tea.* Page 10: *A group of Sockeye salmon, red and ready to spawn, swim up a creek near Iliamna Lake.* Page 12-13: *A sea of lily pads cover a lake at the headwaters of Silver Salmon Creek in Lake Clark National Park and Preserve.* Page 176: *Hundreds of attendees at Salmonstock (now Salmonfest) join together to form a piece of living art designed by Mavis Muller.* Back cover photo: *The crew of the F/V Chulyen tosses out the first buoy during a commercial Sockeye salmon opener in the Ugashik District.*

Publisher: Helen Cherullo
Project Manager: Mary Metz
Acquisitions and Developmental Editor: Deb Easter
Content and Copy Editor: Amy Smith Bell
Cover and Book Designer: Jane Jeszeck, www.jigsawdesign.com
Development and Communications: Lace Thornberg
Cartographer: Ani Rucki
Scientific Advisor: Jack A. Stanford

A catalog record for this book is available at the Library of Congress
ISBN: 978-1-59485-773-7